TORONTO, MISSISSIPPI & JEWEL

JOAN MACLEOD

Playwrights Canada Press
Toronto

Playwrights Canada Press is the publishing imprint of
the Playwrights Union of Canada (PUC): 54 Wolseley St., 2nd fl.,
Toronto, Ontario CANADA M5T 1A5
Tel. (416) 947-0201 Fax. (416) 947-0159

Playwrights Canada Press operates with the generous assistance of
The Canada Council - Writing and Publishing Section, and Theatre Section,
and the Ontario Arts Council.

Front cover photo by Michael Cooper.
Edited by Tony Hamill.

Canadian Cataloguing in Publication Data
MacLeod, Joan, 1954 –
      Toronto, mississippi & jewel
Two plays
ISBN 0-88754-474-6
I. Title.II Title: Jewel
PS8575. L46T67 1989   C812'.54   C89-094003-7
PR9199.3.M3T67 1989

First edition: May 1989.
Second printing: Sept. 1991
Third printing: September 1993
Printed by Hignell Printing Ltd., Winnipeg, Manitoba, Canada.

CONTENTS

Preface

These two plays were written with the generous support of the
Canada Council, the Ontario Arts Council and the Banff Centre.

I am also indebted to the Tarragon Playwrights' Unit where
Toronto, Mississippi was written and to my director and
dramaturge Andy McKim. And finally to my friend and artistic
director Urjo Kareda — his support is extraordinary and to him
I am most grateful.

J.M.

TORONTO, MISSISSIPPI

For Michelle, Bill and Alan
and in loving memory of Dan.

Toronto, Mississippi premiered at Tarragon Theatre in Toronto, October 6, 1987 with the following cast:

JHANA	*Brooke Johnson*
KING	*Bruce McFee*
MADDIE	*Marlane O'Brien*
BILL	*Jim Warren*

Directed by Andy McKim.
Set and costume design by Sue LePage.
Lighting design by Louise Guinand.
Stage manager — Beth Bruck.

Toronto, Mississippi was subsequently produced by the Touchstone Theatre Company in Vancouver, November 11, 1988 with the following cast:

JHANA	*Megan Leitch*
KING	*Peter Blackwood*
MADDIE	*Meredith Bain Woodward*
BILL	*Allan Morgan*

Directed by Roy Surette.
Set design by Helen Jarvis.
Costumes by James Glen and Nancy Tait.
Lighting design by Rebekah Johnson.
Stage manager — Ingrid Turk.

The Characters

KING, *forty, Elvis impersonator, Jhana's father.*

JHANA, *eighteen, moderately mentally handicapped, hyper-active, with symptoms of autism, employed at sheltered workshop.*

BILL, *thirty, poet, part-time college instructor, boarding with Jhana and Maddie.*

MADDIE, *forty, high school English teacher, Jhana's mother.*

The Setting

A middle-class living room in Toronto.

The Running Time

Two acts of approximately one hour each.

Author's Note

In Jhana's first scene she is slightly "rocking back and forth". It's something she does to comfort herself, and a signal to Bill that she's phasing out a little. This is what Maddie refers to later as stimming out and considers inappropriate.

Later in this scene Jhana (pronounced Jah [like jazz] -nah) says "We'll all be at workshop... We'll all be at drop-in." The social circle mentally handicapped people move in is often quite small — the same people Jhana went to school with she now works with, bowls with, and goes to drop-in with — a Friday night event for handicapped people at the local community centre.

Jhana later says "I am mentally handicapped". This is something she does not like having to say but is told to. In this case she becomes angry with her mum for making her say it and she yells, "Close the patio door!" Jhana is imitating something her mum said earlier but it's the emotion behind the phrase she's imitating rather than the meaning — something she does often.

Jhana whines off-stage about finding her clothes, vacuuming etc. She is being very lazy about the way she speaks — partly because she finds the tasks at hand uninteresting but also because her mum understands her even when she's talking 'silly'. If you had to say all your sentences backwards for the next half hour it would be very difficult concentrated work and in a way this is what Jhana has to do all the time. The way she talks naturally is very jumbled but when she is interested in communicating well she can do it; at the very end of the play when she dials 911 she speaks in perfect sentences.

Jhana is also obsessed about her dad coming because she loves him and hasn't seen him for a while. But this carrying one thought at a time rather than a half dozen at once is also part of her mental handicap and comes up often. Jhana often repeats the last line of what her dad is saying — she does this to show she is interested but doesn't have a clue what is being talked about. She'll repeat, she'll agree, she'll imitate the emotion she picks up from that person. Her dad talks over her head because he doesn't live with her.

When Jhana says "Betty died" she refers to the fact that some of the people she went to school with and worked with also have physical handicaps and sometimes a shorter life span. Jhana doesn't have this problem but she is much more accustomed to death than the average eighteen-year-old.

The best way to approach Jhana is to find the Jhana within — she's just like any eighteen-year-old but not as slick and once that discovery's happened there are some mentally handicapped traits that can be added. There is often a flatness to a mentally handicapped person's speech or inappropriate emphasis because what's being said isn't always understood — statements become questions and vice-versa. Physically there's "stimming out" and inappropriate physical behaviour. Mentally handicapped people also often have high anxiety rates and low self-esteem; think of a job interview you don't feel qualified for but you fake your way through.

Jhana is hyper-active, her energy is nearly always unrelenting, she is mentally handicapped with only some symptoms of autism — so don't think of Jhana as autistic.

Jhana is based partially on a friend of mine who is a very lovely mentally handicapped woman. The most important thing I can tell you about playing Jhana is that a mental handicap or any handicap is a sad thing but this life, this particular person is also a joy.

Prologue

Black on set, spot on KING *at microphone, costumed like early Elvis, with a Memphis accent.*

KING   Mrs. Priscilla Presley has just left the building and believe you me folks, that is something we can all be grateful for. So now we can kick our heels up, have a good time. I thank you all for coming out tonight but before I begin a big hello to a special someone who's sitting out there front row centre. I mean, friends and women — they come and go. They certainly have been marching away from me at a steady rate these days. But children... well it's just a very precious thing to have a child. Ladies and gentlemen, my daughter, my little girl — Lisa Marie Presley. Stand up honey, don't be scared. She's still real little so let's treat her nice, let's make her feel right at home.

Black out, KING *exits, lights up on set.*

Act One, Scene One

> JHANA *is dancing full out to loud, early*
> *Elvis music. Eventually she sits and*
> *begins rocking back and forth in a trance-*
> *like manner,* BILL *stops her rocking,*
> *turns off the music.*

BILL   You be Priscilla and I'll be Elvis...

JHANA   I'm Elvis Presley!

BILL   Five minutes on nine one one and then's it's
bed. Deal?

JHANA   I'm Elvis Presley!

BILL   You're always Elvis. How about being Lisa
Marie?

JHANA   No. Bill's Priscilla. It's funny. Right?

BILL   Why can't we both be Elvis? I hate being
her.

JHANA   She isn't dead.

BILL   Good point. So you be Priscilla....

JHANA   You're hating nine one one, right?

BILL   Five minutes. When your mum gives us shit
              for staying up half the night, you can amaze
              her with nine one one. *(role playing Elvis)* I
              smell something burning, Cilla. If Graceland
              burnt....? Lawdy, lawdy... C'mon, Jhana.

JHANA   I'm Elvis Presley!

BILL   Alright. You win. *(role playing Priscilla)*
              Elvis? How many of those pills did you
              take? You hear me? Are you sick honey?
              El?

JHANA   Hi, Bill.

BILL   The name's Priscilla.

JHANA   *(role playing Elvis)* Hi, Priscilla. You're
              funny, right?

BILL   I'm perfectly fine but you look a little rough.
              Half dead if you want to know the truth. I
              don't care if you're Elvis Presley or the
              President of the United States. I'm gonna
              call you an ambulance. Now how on earth
              do you suppose I do that?

JHANA   Nine one one.

BILL   Show me.

JHANA   Nine one one. On her telephone. Pick it up.

BILL   The whole phone?

JHANA   Bill! *(picks up receiver and offers it to* BILL)

BILL   Dial it.

JHANA   Why?

BILL   Look, Jhana. This isn't my idea of a great time either. But you were the one that was all keen on doing this course.

JHANA   She hates it.

BILL   It's only one night a week. You get to hang out at a college, meet guys, learn all kinds of stuff that...

JHANA   It's hard.

BILL   C'mon. You're meeting some new people there, right?

JHANA   We'll all be at the workshop.

BILL   No new faces?

JHANA   We'll all be at drop-in.

BILL   So it's the same old crowd. Lots of old friends there. Right? And lifeskills is valuable stuff...

JHANA   *(pointing to television)* The Loveboat's inside.

BILL   It's not on. You were about to call an ambulance before the King of Rock n' Roll blew up or passed out... sssshhh! That's her.

JHANA   That's her.

                JHANA *dives onto the couch, covers herself with blanket and pretends to be asleep.* MADDIE *enters.*

BILL   How was it?

MADDIE   Lousy. Why's she down here? It's past
       midnight, Bill.

BILL   She fell asleep.

MADDIE   Faker.

BILL   We were watching The Love Boat. I didn't
       like him much when he picked you up.
       Where'd he take you?

MADDIE   Downtown. Why's she breathing heavy?

BILL   Filthy dreams.

MADDIE   She's faking. Jhana?

BILL   Didn't you ever pretend you were sleeping
       when you were little?

MADDIE   She's eighteen years old...

BILL   So that someone would carry you up to bed?
       Or better yet, you'd be visiting somewhere
       and get carried out to the car.

MADDIE   This guy tonight. He wasn't one hundred
       percent horrible. You two have something in
       common.

BILL   That's impossible.

MADDIE   He writes poetry.

BILL   Everybody's a poet. We'd be visiting my
       grandfather's place. He wore this black patch
       on his eye and I used to think this tunnel of
       air went right through his head.

MADDIE   C'mon Jhana.

BILL   He'd carry me outside to my dad's truck.
          The yard smelled like hay and I don't know
          — toilets.

JHANA   *(sits up suddenly)* Toilets!

MADDIE   Faking all along.

JHANA   Princie's gone Mum, right? *(runs to door)*
          Bye-bye!

MADDIE   It's October, Jhana. Close the patio door!

JHANA   Close the patio door!

MADDIE   Up to bed now, okay?

JHANA   Okay?

MADDIE   Did you clean your room?

JHANA   Did you clean your room?

MADDIE   DID YOU CLEAN YOUR ROOM?

JHANA   Yes.

MADDIE   And brushed your teeth?

JHANA   Yes. And brushed your teeth. Princie's dead
          now, Mum.

MADDIE   We're all aware of that.

JHANA   Elvis Presley was on the bus?

MADDIE   No more nonsense.

JHANA   Not Daddy.

MADDIE   Good night, Jhana.

JHANA   The man on the bus is gone?

MADDIE   Who is the man on the bus?

JHANA   Who is the man on the bus?

MADDIE   And quit the copying. Did you meet someone on the bus today?

JHANA   Yes.

MADDIE   Who?

JHANA   Princie.

MADDIE   I'm not kidding around here, Jhana. Who did you meet?

JHANA   Elvis Presley.

BILL   Elvis Presley on the Woodbine Bus? Quick, call the National Enquirer.

MADDIE   Bill, just let me handle this, alright?

JHANA   Number nine. Number two. The Woodbine Bus!

MADDIE   Did you talk to someone on the bus today?

JHANA   Yes I did!

MADDIE   Someone from the workshop? You talked to a man? A man you didn't know?

JHANA   Yes.

MADDIE   Did he touch you?

BILL   A new record —

JHANA   Oh Yes!

BILL   ...for jumping the gun.

> *Bill arranges two chairs, one behind the other.*

MADDIE   Show me where he touched you.

JHANA   Black hair.

MADDIE   He touched your hair? Bloody social workers. I knew you weren't ready for bus training...

BILL   Okay. I'm the man on the bus.

JHANA   Hi, Billy.

BILL   No. I'm the man on the bus.

JHANA   Hi.

BILL   Hello there.

JHANA   Hello there black hair.

BILL   I'm the man on the bus with black hair. You just get off work honey?

JHANA   Elvis Presley.

BILL   I'm the man on the bus and I look like Elvis Presley?

JHANA	Yes!
BILL	And you like me?
JHANA	*(touching his hair)* Black hair.
BILL	You touch my nice black hair...
JHANA	Yes!
BILL	Do I touch you?
JHANA	No!
BILL	I don't like it when you touch me. SHE molested him, Maddie.
MADDIE	How many times have I told you? What is the only thing we can say on the bus? What do we know from memory?
JHANA	From memory... January 8, 1935. Tupelo, Mississippi!
MADDIE	Great. My daughter is going to go bussing off to Niagara Falls by mistake one day, chanting Elvis Presley's birthday. Damn your father.
JHANA	Elvis Presley's birthday!
MADDIE	What have we gone over six hundred times in the past three months. Jhana? C'mon... I am...
JHANA & MADDIE	I am Jhana Kelly...
JHANA	I live at three nine two Chisholm Avenue...

MADDIE   Three two nine.

JHANA   Three two nine...

MADDIE   I am...

JHANA   I am lost.

MADDIE   I am...

JHANA   I am lost.

MADDIE   And? I am...

JHANA   I am mentally handicapped...

MADDIE   Please help...

JHANA   Please help me find my way home! *(rocks back and forth)*

MADDIE   Now show me the paper. Where's your purse?

BILL   Lighten up, Maddie.

                JHANA *dumps out the contents of her purse, finding lipstick and applying it meticulously.*

MADDIE   Quit stalling, Jhana.

BILL   She's been working at getting that on straight for weeks.

MADDIE   And we've been working at bussing since March.

BILL   Goodnight. *(exits)*

MADDIE   The address, Jhana. It should be written
                down on the yellow paper and in your purse.
                I'm very upset with...

JHANA   Close the patio door!

                        Black.

Act One, Scene Two

The next morning.

BILL   There is no way you slept through last night.

MADDIE   Good morning to you too, Bill.

BILL   We were all assaulted by Donovan at three
                    o'clock this morning. I mean he was terrible
                    twenty years ago. What if he's having a
                    comeback? *(places finger on Adam's apple)*
                    Hurdy Gurdy Man. The volume made my
                    teeth vibrate. Donovan.

JHANA   *(off)* Mum? The socks are dead. Princie
                    took a new house. Where's the drawer?

MADDIE   In my room. I just folded everything.
                    Wear some socks the same colour as your
                    T-shirt.

BILL   Then at about five they were all out on the
                    front porch throwing up and yelling in this
                    made-up language... like tongues. Have you
                    ever noticed that a lot of cabs come and go
                    from there? Maybe it's an after hours place
                    or a whorehouse.

MADDIE	We were always the noisy neighbours — for years. You can imagine living next door to someone like King.
JHANA	*(off)* Mum? The socks are laundried too. Where?
MADDIE	In the clothes basket, Jhana. All paired up.
JHANA	All paired up. Who's vacuuming on there now?
MADDIE	You are. The whole upstairs.
JHANA	Why?
MADDIE	Because I said so. We all pitch in.
JHANA	We all pitch in, Bill!
BILL	He called last night.
MADDIE	Who?
BILL	The King of Rock n' Roll. He called last night betwen sets.
MADDIE	He's in town?
BILL	Buffalo. At the Holiday Inn.
MADDIE	The Holiday Inn? You're joking.
BILL	He wants Jhana to come down for the show tonight.

MADDIE   Just like that.

BILL   He didn't talk to her; he wanted to check it
                out with you first.

MADDIE   She's supposed to get there all on her own?

BILL   She can bribe the driver on the Woodbine
                Bus...

MADDIE   Did he sound alright?

                (JHANA *enters*)

BILL   King said to remind you that he is her father
                and hasn't seen her since June.

JHANA   Her father. Where's Daddy on?

MADDIE   He's in Buffalo.

JHANA   On Buffalo. Where's Daddy on coming here?

BILL   He wants you to go see him. He's not here.
                He's in another city called Buffalo.

JHANA   Okay. C'mon. Buffalo.

MADDIE   Thanks, Bill.

JHANA   Daddy's on incoming Buffalo. Let's go.

MADDIE   How'd it be if we asked Daddy to come here?

JHANA   Okay!

MADDIE   Bill?

BILL   I'm just a boarder.

MADDIE	We'll phone him when I come home from shopping. He wouldn't be out of bed yet.
JHANA	Okay. Phoning Daddy!
MADDIE	When I come home.
JHANA	C'mon.
MADDIE	When I come home from shopping. And when you finish vacuuming.
JHANA	Okay. Bill's on the vacuum too. In helping.
BILL	I'll give you a hand. If you'll do some of the dusting.
JHANA	And you'll do some of the dusting! Daddy's on incoming Buffalo. Here! *(exits)*
MADDIE	We'll ask him for tomorrow. He should have Sunday off.
JHANA	*(off)* Okay!
BILL	When was the last time you saw him?
MADDIE	Easter. I took Jhana up to Ottawa. He looked lousy, kind of overweight.
BILL	Elvis in his later years. What a dedicated impersonator.
MADDIE	He only does the early stuff. In fact, he's the only one who does early Elvis. He thinks Presley really died when he signed with RCA. Did you tell him I was out with someone last night?

BILL   Did you want me to?

MADDIE   Isn't that stupid? We haven't lived together for nearly a decade but I still love turning that knife. Just a tad.

BILL   I told him you were out with a brilliant young poet.

MADDIE   David?

BILL   Top of the line.

MADDIE   David owns a chain of drycleaning stores.

BILL   Pretty tough competition — the King of Rock n' Roll.

MADDIE   David isn't competing with King or anyone else, unfortunately. He's nice enough, but sort of a jerk when it came to Jhana. After he met her, he told me she had a sort of grace — in the bovine sense. He writes poems about nature... as a hobby.

BILL   God help me.

MADDIE   He'd never heard of your book.

BILL   What? The man must live in a cocoon. David the dry cleaning poet. I like that actually. I think all poets should be dry cleaners.

MADDIE   He knows sweet nothing about kids let alone someone like Jhana. I'll be back in an hour. You don't have to worry about cleaning. I've done piss all this week. Okay?

> BILL *nods, and puts early Elvis on
> stereo.* MADDIE *exits.* JHANA *comes
> running in.*

JHANA   Daddy's on Buffalo!

BILL   Yes, ma'am. Before this song ends you and I are going to do the fastest dusting job ever.

JHANA   Okay.

> BILL *and* JHANA *dust to the music.*
> JHANA *dances and imitates Elvis.*

BILL   Remember how your mum got so pissed off last night about not having the paper in your purse?

JHANA   The paper in your purse. It's in a new house, Bill. On Buffalo. Daddy's on Buffalo. In Princie's mouth.

BILL   Maybe it's lost.

JHANA   Maybe it's lost.

BILL   So what we're gonna do is copy out your name, address and phone number. I'll do the printing if you tell me what to say. Agreed?

JHANA   Okay.

BILL   So, do you have a name or what?

JHANA   Jhana.

BILL   I want the whole thing.

JHANA   Jhana Gladys Kelly.

BILL   You got a phone number Gladys? I might
               want to ring you up sometime. I might want
               to take you on a date.

JHANA   Okay.

BILL   I might want to take you for a beer. Or to a
               rock concert. How do I do it? What's your
               phone number Jhana Gladys Kelly?

JHANA   692-4444.

BILL   Good. I'll call. What if I want to come to
               your house. Where do you live?

JHANA   Here.

BILL   I need an address, angel.

JHANA   I live at... I live at three, nine, three, nine,
               three, nine. I live at three TWO nine
               Chisholm Avenue.

BILL   You're a wizard.

JHANA   Wizard. She's out on a date. Out on a date
               on Buffalo.

BILL   What city do you live in?

JHANA   Buffalo.

BILL   Nope.

JHANA   Chisholm Avenue. Tupelo. Tupelo,
               Mississippi.

BILL	Toronto, angel.
JHANA	Toronto, angel. Toronto, Mississippi.
BILL	Close.
JHANA	You're Andrew, right?
BILL	Never heard of him.
JHANA	At her workshop. Me and Andrew. He's funny, right?
BILL	Andrew's a guy you work with?
JHANA	He's funny. He's drying my face after lunch. Being tall. Right?
BILL	If you say so. You like this guy?
JHANA	Okay. You're Andrew, right? For pretend, Bill.
BILL	Okay. But no funny stuff, Jhana Gladys. You got that? It's after work and we're just talking. In a cafe. Okay?
JHANA	Yes.
BILL	So what'll you have? You wanna beer?
JHANA	Diet coke please thank you.
BILL	C'mon. Have a beer. You're old enough.
JHANA	Okay.
BILL	Wow. You give in real easy. Wanna go to bed? Wanna get married?

JHANA   Okay.

BILL   No, Jhana. Not okay. It's our first date.
               Alright?

JHANA   Diet coke please thank you.

BILL   You live at home?

JHANA   Chisholm Avenue.

BILL   You don't talk much. Can't you ask me a
               thing or two?

JHANA   Okay.

BILL   *(pause)* So...

JHANA   Princie's not south. Buffalo or that. He's
               dead. Right?

BILL   Can't follow you.

JHANA   He's not on the patio. Not sleeping. It's
               sunny in his back. Princie.

BILL   Who the hell's Princie?

JHANA   Her dog.

BILL   Whose dog?

JHANA   Jhana Gladys Kelly. Chisholm Avenue.

BILL   Repeat after me: Princie was my dog. He's
               dead.

JHANA   Princie was my...

BILL	Jesus, what am I saying. You're not supposed to talk about death on a first date. It's against the rules.
JHANA	You're not allowed, Bill!
BILL	So sweetheart, you like working alright?
JHANA	Sweetheart.
BILL	What do you do exactly?
JHANA	Fine thank you.
BILL	Right.
JHANA	Right! *(pause)* Sweetheart.
BILL	You hungry?
JHANA	*(rehearsed)* Do you like Italian food?
BILL	Sure. Pizza and that is pretty...
JHANA	*(rehearsed)* I like it very much.
BILL	Terrific. We'll eat a kingsize.
JHANA	Daddy wears the suits. Right? You don't wear them. Only black. Don't wear a white suit.
BILL	Whatever you say. This is great pizza. You like it?
JHANA	Diet coke please thank you.
BILL	Top of the line. *(suddenly choking and coughing)* Jesus! It went down the wrong way. Help me.

JHANA   Sweetheart.

BILL   Do something. Please!

JHANA   Andrew's being funny. He's being tall.

BILL   Call someone! What the hell's that number?

JHANA   Nine... She hates nine one one!

BILL   I'm dying here, Jhana. How am I gonna date you again?

JHANA   *(picks up receiver)* Nine one one on Bill! *(slams it down)*

BILL   That's not how you do it. Okay, fine. Andrew just bought it on an olive. His heart was broken. Death by dating. The defunct Andrew.

                     JHANA *turns on the stereo.*

BILL   Off. Right now, Jhani. You wanna hear about my first love? I was around your age. No. I was sixteen but looked forty. Her name was Diane and she was eighteen and divorced. She also had a dead sister — car wreck I think — which made Diane quite famous locally.

JHANA   Headphones, Bill.

BILL   I'm spilling my guts here. You know Jhana, if Elvis' last girlfriend had taken a lifeskills telephone course, the King of Rock n' Roll might still be with us. And your father would be making his living singing "Light My Fire".

JHANA   No more nine one one!

BILL   Okay. Headphones are swell.

                    JHANA *puts on headphones and sings phrases of songs, hums.*

BILL   Actually Diane and I barely made it past kissing. She was hoping to get back together with her ex. He was haywire. You can read all about it in my first collection: Love And The Need For Firearms, unpublished.

JHANA   *(singing)* Shake, shake and roll.
                    Shake, shake and roll.

BILL   Oh. It's the first roll in the hay you want to hear about. That's easy... some creature I picked up at the library. I was twenty-seven. She was around ninety. Not romantic enough for you? Well screw you then, Miss Raw Sexual Energy. No doubt you'll jump another passenger on the Woodbine Bus and give him the business.

JHANA   Hi, Bill.

BILL   Hi, angel. Your first time will happen in the best way possible. Where should we make it? July on Yonge Street. Just getting dark. He'll be from ...Kenora. Better yet, Lake-of-the-Woods. No. Fuck the northern stuff. He's from Etobicoke and sensitive. Maybe it really will be this Andrew. He'll be a complete wizard when it comes to money — counts back his change. Knows what colour means what amount. Jhana and Andrew — a regular pair. So don't shut down. When Andrew feels your skin, hair, all those hidden and rough places — he'll be able to re-make the entire world.

                    Black.

Act One, Scene Three

A spot is up on KING, *costumed like Elvis, at microphone, singing an early Elvis song. Lights then go down on* KING *and up on set, the next night.*

JHANA   The celery is late. Before dinner, Bill. You going to eat it? Like Daddy? *(shows him plate of celery sticks)*

BILL   Did you make that?

JHANA   Yes.

BILL   What's inside there? It looks like porridge.

JHANA   Cheese, Bill. In Daddy's mouth. Where is it lately?

MADDIE   The celery and cheese are perfect. We will eat them before dinner when your father gets here. He isn't late, Jhana. He'll be here in half an hour.

JHANA	Half an hour. He isn't here now.
BILL	Shortly. You look pretty. Is that your dad on your shirt or the real Elvis?
JHANA	Yes. Princie isn't here. He's dead, Bill.
BILL	Sure is.
JHANA	I'm pretty.
BILL	You're absolutely gorgeous. You're gonna knock him out.
JHANA	Knock him out! Mum? He isn't here. He's on the stereo. *(puts on Elvis record)*
MADDIE	This is your father's day off, Jhana. I bet the last thing he wants to hear right now is Elvis Presley. Put on one of Bill's Donovan records. He keeps them under his pillow.
BILL	Liar.
JHANA	Liar, Bill. Daddy isn't listening. Is he?
MADDIE	Maybe you should start calling him Dad. Daddy sounds babyish. Don't you think?
JHANA	Don't you think Bill?
MADDIE	Try it out. 'Hi, Dad. Nice to see you'.
JHANA	Hi, Dad. Nice to see you Dad. Celery Dad. By me. Bill is dead. Dad.
BILL	I am not! Maybe a little tired but...

JHANA	Bill is maybe a little tired Dad. *(turns up stereo)*
MADDIE	Turn it down! Now Jhana.

JHANA *puts on headphones.*

MADDIE	Did you buy the wine?
BILL	In the fridge.

KING *enters, wearing regular clothes, carrying a short white cape covered in sequins and an overnight bag.*

MADDIE	Good Lord. We have a doorbell you know.
KING	Sssshhhh... *(sneaking up on* JHANA *and wrapping cape around her)*
JHANA	Daddy! This is yours too?
MADDIE	*(whispering)* Say Dad, Jhana.
KING	Hi, Maddie.
MADDIE	You two remember each other?
BILL	We met last winter when I moved in.
KING	Right. How's it going?
BILL	Splendid.
KING	You got a new haircut, Jhana. It's great.
JHANA	It's great, Dad. This is mine, Dad? *(referring to cape)* Elvis Presley is here! He's on my back.

MADDIE   Nice cape.

KING   Some fan gave it to me.

MADDIE   Is the show going okay? I read a review in
                the Buffalo paper.

KING   You bought a Buffalo paper? That's nice
                Maddie.

MADDIE   It's good.

JHANA   It's good, Dad. And it's celery. Made for by
                me. Dad.

                BILL *reaches for a piece of celery.*

JHANA   Don't!

MADDIE   Your Dad can't eat a whole plate. It's for
                everyone.

JHANA   Eat it Bill too. Okay, Dad?

KING   Okay. How's school, Jhana?

JHANA   It's working.

MADDIE   Jhani's doing her first placement at a
                workshop — assembly stuff.

KING   Good for you darling. You building cars?

JHANA   Okay. You hate it, Dad.

KING   What?

JHANA   The workshop. You're with the screws in a
                bag. Screws in a bag. Four of them in a
                bag.

BILL	Wine?
JHANA	Okay. *(referring to cape)* We're beautiful Dad.
MADDIE	Just one glass, Jhana. Me too, Bill. Thanks.

        BILL *exits.*

KING	So you put four screws in one bag. What else?
JHANA	Lunch.
KING	And?
JHANA	Coffee. Twice. With Andrew?
KING	Who's Andrew.
JHANA	The boy there. You're liking him, Dad? And me? You're gonna sing?
KING	Maybe after I have a drink. Maybe after supper.
MADDIE	Where's the tour going?
KING	Eastern states. Detroit after this. I brought a list in case anything comes up. You alright, Madelaine?
MADDIE	Fine. Eat your celery, Dad. Jhana's sort of screwing up at the workshop. Right?
KING	Why?
MADDIE	Probably bored. If she does okay there are some great programs she could get into. Jhana? No Elvis, okay? Put on something quiet.

JHANA	Okay Dad?
KING	Fine. Is school alright?
MADDIE	Same as ever. My grade twelve class is good. Bill's come in a couple of times. He did his thesis on Margaret Atwood, so that's a help. I don't know. I guess I'm a little tired of it.

BILL *enters with wine and newspaper.*

KING	Can I see that paper?
BILL	'An invigorating and nostalgic look at...'
KING	I hate that nostalgia shit. That's not why I'm up there.
BILL	But it's a great review. If my last one was half that good...
MADDIE	You've been reviewed more than once?
BILL	Not in the strictest sense but...
KING	I thought you were a professor.
BILL	T.A. One course.
MADDIE	Bill's published a book of poetry. It's very good.
KING	I didn't know people still wrote poetry.
JHANA	*(handing him book)* This is Bill. Dad.
BILL	And I didn't know people would still come out for Elvis.

KING   For eternity man. Wow. Some picture. I mean it's good and looks like you but it's like there's this knife in your gut. Sixty-eight pages.

MADDIE   That's normal for poetry.

KING   At eleven ninety-five. You must be making a mint.

BILL   There is a knife in my gut.

MADDIE   There's a sequence in there called "Black Morning" that's made Bill a bit of a celebrity. In fact he's doing a reading from it this week... it's been anthologized, twice... I'm going to check on dinner. *(exits)*

KING   How many copies you sell?

BILL   Thirty-seven.

JHANA   Bill's on the book Dad.

KING   He sure is. That's great man. Poetry. "The Path Of Despair". What do you know.

BILL   I teach, you know, in Canadian Studies. Literature.

KING   Right.

BILL   Animal as victim, environment as victim, women as victim. That sort of thing. Despair's more of a sideline. Not that they don't overlap. I love women's literature. And it's very despairing, for the most part. This is a very exciting time for female writers in this country. I mean since the time I was born.

KING   Why would that be?

BILL   They just haven't had much of a voice at all, up until now —

KING   Unhappy women have always tended to speak loud and clear around me.

BILL   Right.

KING   I'm out there last night, just talking. And this woman, she's right at the front at this table with two other ladies.

JHANA tries to sit on his knee.

KING   That's kinda heavy, darling. How about you and me just holding hands for a while? This woman was real heavy. All dolled up and fat. And sad! Man. I wasn't even half way through the first set and she started. Just weeping at first but then full-blown. Hyperventilating tears. Just sobbing away.

BILL   Don't you just get up and sing and shake your hips?

KING   No, I don't.

JHANA   No, Bill.

MADDIE   *(off)* I think we're about ready to eat. Can you give me a hand, Jhana?

JHANA   No.

KING   Help your Mum, sweetheart. That's the stuff.

JHANA exits.

BILL	I watched Blue Hawaii when I was about seven.
KING	You got a girlfriend?
BILL	Of sorts.
KING	What's "of sorts"? She half fish or something?
BILL	You do sing and shake and that most of the time. Right?
KING	I sing... tell stories. I have re-invented the man; put all the parts back together in a way better suited to survive. He didn't have a very thick skin.
BILL	Thus the weight.
KING	You almost ready out there?
MADDIE	*(off)* Just about.
JHANA	*(off)* Just about, Dad.
BILL	How many of you are there?
KING	Playing the King? Not so many as before. Probably about the same as the number of people writing poetry. Sixty-eight pages. That's a son-of-a-bitch. Don't you think?
BILL	I suppose.

KING (in a Memphis accent) We're in Texas. Way
the hell in the middle of nowhere. Very hot.
I've been driving. Sonny and Red are in the
back and some asshole we've just met is in
the front with me. He's making us stop every
twenty minutes or so — taking a piss, taking
a picture. There are these clouds in the east,
big and thick. Did I say this sort of thing has
happened before? I have heard the voice of
God twice: once through a blackbird, out
back at Graceland, another time while
holding a gun against the head of a woman.
This is what's whispered while taking aim,
"I'm listening. I wasn't before but now I'm
all yours."

But this is different man. I am looking at
these clouds because they are, you know,
pretty good. They're moving fast. Heading
south. But when I stare them down, they
stop. When I look back toward home, they
come with me. I direct those clouds across
the whole fucking sky.

Every dream I've ever dreamed has come true
a hundred times. I'm always the hero. None
of this surprises me.

Black.

Act One, Scene Four

After supper the same night, BILL *and* KING *show the first signs of drunkeness.*

KING   When you were little, Jhana, around five years old...

JHANA   Five years old, Dad?

KING   We had this old van, all painted up in rainbows and psychedelic shit. I washed it about forty times a week and I'd put you inside...

JHANA   Yes!

KING   Aim the hose at that pretty face behind the windshield. Remember?

JHANA   Remember?

KING   And you'd fake that I'd knocked you over. You'd ring the water out of your pigtails. Born performers, you and me.

JHANA   You and me, Dad.

KING   Remember touring sweetheart? The three of us and the band driving across the country? Naw, you were too little then.

JHANA   I'm too little, Dad.

KING   Drink up there, Bill.

BILL   Yes sir.

KING   Maddie?

MADDIE   Yeah. More. This was my favourite. Driving to Edmonton in the middle of the night. It was about two hundred below and we stopped for coffee...

KING   The Diamond Kitchen.

MADDIE   You remember the horses?

KING   Bunched up around the fence.

BILL   Why would they be outside if it was so cold?

KING   This is the wild west man! Jhani's real small and I'm holding her inside this sleeping bag.

JHANA   Me.

KING   You're checking out this big black horse. It's crazy looking and rough 'cause of winter. You're face to face. You just reach out and touch his nose, no fear, none whatsoever.

MADDIE   You thought the Northern Lights were about the funniest thing ever invented. You'd point at them...

KING   Then just about pee yourself laughing.

JHANA   Pee yourself laughing!

BILL   You know I've been up north too but the best view I ever had of the lights was from Southern Ontario.

KING   *(pause)* What do you know.

MADDIE   Really.

JHANA   Really, Bill.

KING   *(in the Memphis accent)* This dog sleeps on
                the porch all day but when night comes he's
                got a whole life of his own. Man that's
                great. Just like us. We're driving through
                night in this big sonofabitch. Nobody knows
                what we're doing. Not even the ole boys in
                the back seat.

JHANA   Elvis Presley!

KING   *(same accent)* The one and only, darling.

JHANA   You gonna sing for her?

KING   Who?

JHANA   Jhana Kelly.

                KING *sings one verse of "Are You*
                Lonesome Tonight?" then JHANA *cuts*
                him off.

JHANA   Sing faster!

KING   *(singing)* You may go to college, You may go
                to school,

                JHANA *tries to sing "baby, baby, baby"*
                in the background

KING   You may have a pink Cadillac
                But don't you be nobody's fool.
                Come back baby come back,
                Come back baby come back,
                Come back baby I want
                To play house with you.

MADDIE   Good night, Jhana.

JHANA   *(to* KING*)* You're sleeping with me?

KING   No ma'am. But I'll make you breakfast.

JHANA   Dad's making breakfast, Bill.

BILL   Good.

JHANA   Mum? You're sleeping with Bill?

MADDIE   I don't sleep with Bill. I sleep in my own bed. Quit stalling, Jhana. You're being silly. Your Dad is staying down here. Everything else is the same as ever.

JHANA   The same as ever.

KING   C'mon you. Show me your room. Show me what you look like sleeping.

             JHANA *and* KING *exit.*

BILL   I like him, Maddie.

MADDIE   No you don't.

BILL   Why didn't you say he was staying overnight here?

MADDIE   It's no big deal.

BILL   Divorced pals. I think that's wonderful. I really do. *(holds up bottle)* Is there more?

MADDIE   We're all out.

BILL   Maybe you'll be like Elizabeth Taylor...
marry the same guy twice. Or Zsa Zsa
Gabor. Didn't she do that? You mean we're
all out of alcohol? Completely? I'll get
more.

MADDIE   It's nearly midnight. And it's Sunday.

BILL   In case you hadn't noticed, Maddie, we have
a liquor store right next door.

MADDIE   You're going to buy liquor from the
neighbours? That's really low, Bill.

BILL   I can probably buy all sorts of things there.
What would you like? Beer? Heroin?
Perhaps a film...

MADDIE   You're really serious.

BILL   More white wine? King seems to like it and
he's an alcoholic.

MADDIE   He has it under control. You, on the other
hand, are acting like a lunatic.

BILL   If I don't come back...

MADDIE   Bill? You are okay aren't you? You seem
really...

BILL   Fun loving.

MADDIE   I'm serious, Willie...

       BILL *exits,* KING *enters.*

KING   Where's Lord Byron gone?

MADDIE	Hunting down more liquor.
KING	Jhana's real wired, eh?
MADDIE	What else is new.
KING	But great. You're doing a great job and all. Always have.
MADDIE	She's really screwing up at this workshop.
KING	Everyone screws up at their first job.
MADDIE	I didn't.
KING	**You making it with Mr. Despair?**
MADDIE	People think certain words work magic — group home, workshop. They hear that and assume everything's taken care of. Someone from York just did a research project on her. She's moderately mentally handicapped — moderate. I like that, like the weather when we lived on the coast. Superbly dyslexic... very complicated version of it. Symptoms of autism or soft autism. That's what they're saying now. That's the style. There is a style of everything. But then you'd know all about that.
KING	I'm out of style Maddie. I'm the greaser at the end of the row while the rest of you are streaking your hair and buying Volvos... she'll make out.
MADDIE	So you've said. Ever since she was diagnosed.
KING	But it's true, Madelaine. She's done okay.

MADDIE   Bill's great with her. Better than I am, to be perfectly honest. It's not really any of your business, you know, how Bill fits into my life.

KING   My first job was playing a wedding. A lot of the stuff we played through twice because we only knew eight numbers. We'd have been sued except that at weddings everyone's uncle gets pissed and wants to get up on stage and sing "The Impossible Dream". Most bands hate that kind of shit. We encouraged it. You're too hard on yourself about her. You always have been.

MADDIE   I don't have any choice.

KING   You have some...

MADDIE   And don't tell me, King of the Road, about letting things unfold naturally. Her doing okay is a full time job. For me.

KING   You want me to take her for a while?

MADDIE   Right to some motel in Detroit. She needs her routine.

KING   We have a routine.

MADDIE   Drinking, getting up at noon. Is she going to stay in your room? Sleep in a twin bed next to you and some bar fly: Cindy, Lucy-Ann, Tammi with an 'i'. I've always hated the sound of my voice when I talk to you.

KING   There aren't any Cindy-Anns or Tammies right now.

MADDIE	You mean at this particular moment. Here and now. There's probably one or both of them waiting out in the car or in your motel room.
KING	I came on the bus.
MADDIE	I also don't take any of this stuff very seriously anymore. I really don't.
KING	You've made a fist.
MADDIE	Bill delights in making people feel good about themselves. Do you have any idea how great that is for Jhana?
KING	I can imagine.
MADDIE	I mean he's got the confidence of a shoe when it comes to himself but he really does make people feel, you know, pretty good.
KING	He's sort of straight.
MADDIE	Perfect King.
KING	Perfect. *(touching* MADDIE'S *face)*
MADDIE	You're like your daughter, repeating.
KING	You smell good.
MADDIE	Right. Booze and garlic. Lovely stuff.
KING	You smell like you. The way your pillow used to.
MADDIE	Since when did you lie around sniffing my pillow? Since never.

KING   The Diamond Kitchen. We settle that little girl of ours down in the front of the van. The lights have calmed down, left something thick in the air. We make love against the fence post and you got a little cut at the top of your leg.

MADDIE   Your memory is very selective.

KING   There should always be something at risk.

MADDIE   The next morning we had a helluva fight. You'd spent practically our last dime on an amplifier and hadn't even told me or...

KING   Fuck the next morning.

                          MADDIE *and* KING *kiss then hear* BILL *approaching, they stop.* BILL *enters unaware of what has just happened.*

BILL   The very first movie I saw, I mean in a theater, was Blue Hawaii.

KING   So you said. How'd your mission go?

BILL   It was also about the dumbest fucking movie ever made. Even as a little kid, I thought he was dumb. *(producing a bright purple wine from under his coat)*

MADDIE   Oh good. Nothing like a little pancake syrup at the end of a day.

BILL   Moody Blue. Brilliant stuff. Where's the crystal?

                          BILL *exits.*

KING   You look about ready to collapse, lady.

MADDIE   He barely drinks, you know.

                        BILL *enters with tall glasses of wine.*

BILL   You know Maddie? Our neighbours are good
              folk. Real salt of the earth.

MADDIE   You're going to get sick Bill. You get sick
              mixing beer and water. Remember?

BILL   They're just sitting around, watching a little
              TV, skinning live animals, that sort of thing.
              I showed them some poems, explained how I
              was raised by a family of timber wolves, in
              the suburbs of Ottawa.

KING   I told Jhana I'd be up again after New
              Year's.

MADDIE   Then you'd better explain that means you
              won't be there for Christmas.

BILL   So why do you do it? Why glorify... No.
              It's even more bizarre than that. You're a
              human effigy. I mean at least you could
              imitate someone who really was a tragic hero.
              God knows there's enough around.

KING   Elvis was magic man. Pure and simple.

BILL   Wearing diapers at forty? Giving away fleets
              of Cadillacs to strangers? And guns. Didn't
              he spend around a million a week on
              revolvers and...

MADDIE   I'm going to clean up a little.

BILL

(to KING) Why don't you be Sylvia Plath?
"Every woman adores a fascist."

KING

You need a hand?

MADDIE

No. I'm fine. *(exits)*

BILL

And all these phony badges and shit from
Nixon. He was pretty fucked, all around if
you ask me.

KING

(in the Memphis accent) I chased every girl I
ever met. This one girl was fourteen. Her
mother threatened to charge me with rape.
She comes in to talk to me after the show.
You know something? By the end of our
talk, I could've made the mother too.

BILL

You do that very well.

KING

How about some poetry? You write poems
about Jhana?

BILL

No.

KING

I'd love to see something like that lying flat
on a page.

BILL

I don't write poems about Jhana. I live with
her.

KING

She's wearing that cape to bed. That dumb
cape I gave her.

BILL

Sometimes she's in overdrive and it's really
hard to take. She'll be bitchy to Maddie.
Just whining or glued to the TV. She'll talk
about Andrew, this guy she's hot on from
work until you can't stand it anymore.

KING   It's overtop of her nightgown. That dumb
                cape.

                MADDIE *enters.*

MADDIE   I'm ready to call it a night.

KING   I'm pretty shot.

BILL   *(to* MADDIE) You need the blankets and
                stuff out of my room?

MADDIE   It's okay.

BILL   The almighty Elvis. Just a fat old guy, afraid
                to leave his room.

KING   We're all fat and mean, pal. But even the
                biggest jerk in the world, when he tucks his
                kid into bed, he leaves his hand on her
                forehead a minute cause he loves the warmth.

BILL   I don't know how you could do it.

KING   What? Every dream I've dreamed has come
                true a hundred times. That's the bad ones
                too, boy. Nightmares the size of China.
                Going to Jesus. That's what the Southerners
                call self-destruction and they're fucking
                ecstatic about it.

BILL   I don't know how —

KING   They're driving drunk, right out of the
                womb. They're going to Jesus.

BILL   Leaving a kid.

MADDIE   That's between me and King. It's nothing to
                do with Jhana. Or with you.

KING   I'm going upstairs.

MADDIE   I'll be up in a minute.

                  KING *exits.* BILL *is trying to focus on*
                  MADDIE, *he's very drunk.*

MADDIE   I'll see you in the morning. Okay?

BILL   Where is it you're going now? Tell me where
                  it is you're going.

MADDIE   I'm going upstairs.

BILL   Where?

MADDIE   Upstairs.

BILL   Tell me where it is you're going.

MADDIE   You're drunk. Goodnight, Willy.

BILL   What will he do? Why is it his mouth and
                  hands...

MADDIE   You can sleep down here. That might be
                  easier.

                  MADDIE *covers* BILL *with a blanket.*

BILL   You're my family?

MADDIE   I know.

BILL   You'll kiss your family on the mouth?

                  MADDIE *kisses* BILL *quickly on the*
                  forehead.

BILL   Say where it is you're going. Say it after me.

                 Lights fade.

MADDIE   Night. *(heads for stairs)*

BILL   *(singing slightly, gospel style)*
                 I'm going to Jesus
                 I just can't wait
                 running straight to
                 the arms of Jesus

                 Black.

Act Two, Scene One

> *Lights up on* KING *who is drinking milk
> from the carton, preparing to leave;*
> JHANA *, in her nightgown, surprises
> him.*

JHANA   Dad!

KING   Good morning, sweetheart.

JHANA   *(referring to carton)* You're not allowed. I
said you're not.

KING   Yeah? Who are you?

JHANA   Jhana!

KING   You the fridge patrol? Are you hell bent on
justice at any cost?

JHANA   *(imitating* MADDIE) We all have to live here
young lady.

KING   *(in the Memphis accent)* Momma. She'd be
sleeping pretty as sunrise. Right at this
particular moment.

JHANA   Sing.

KING You don't want to hear me sing this early. Trust me. Let me get up now. Okay?

JHANA Why?

KING C'mon.

JHANA You're making her breakfast.

KING I don't know, Jhana. I don't know if there's time.

JHANA I'm helping. Dad.

KING You gonna help me out under the bright lights? Sing for your keep?

JHANA Okay! And dancing. Everyone's clapping for me. At working I sing, at drop-in.

KING Drop out, Jhana. It's our only chance, you and me.

JHANA You and me. Making breakfast. Now.

KING In Windsor I met one of your pals.

JHANA Who?

KING A girl called Bonita.

JHANA My pal! *(pause)* I don't know her, Dad.

KING She had a job cleaning up.

JHANA Steffie cleans up.

KING Does she now. This Bonita...

JHANA	My pal! Can she come here?
KING	Actually you haven't met her before, Jhani.
JHANA	Why?
KING	What I meant is she's like you.
JHANA	I like her too.
KING	So. At any rate, this Bonita, she'd be around forty and lived at the motel. Took care of everything real good. Even combed out the fringe on the carpet. Imagine that.
JHANA	All right.
KING	She'd just about kill herself that I wouldn't do the Hawaiian Wedding Song. She came to the show every night. Requested that song every five minutes or so. Bonita. Not as pretty as you. Nearly as smart though.
JHANA	I'm not smart.
KING	You make out okay though? You don't get teased or that anymore? Some rough patches there when you were little. Bonita. Maybe you'll get a real job one day like her.
JHANA	I have a real job.
KING	Yeah? How much you taking home?
JHANA	Home.
KING	You making any money?
JHANA	I make a pay cheque Dad.

KING   How much?

JHANA   On Fridays. In her purse.

KING   Hawaiian Wedding Song. That's a load of shit to be singing night after night, isn't it?

JHANA   Okay.

KING   I mean I swore I'd never put on one of those jumpsuits and do that trip. I've always just done him clean, Jhani. Sun Record days, good days. But people come out for the white suits and scarves. The Hawaiian Wedding Song. And these are lean times. So your old dad, Jhana, he gave in.

JHANA   Gave in Dad?

KING   That cape I brought you? It was custom made *(beat)* for me. But not anymore. No more white suits.

JHANA   No more white suits!

KING   You got her.

JHANA   No more white suits!

                KING *puts coat on.*

JHANA   Can I come?

KING   No.

JHANA   Where are you going?

KING   After Christmas Jhana, maybe you and me can take off for a few days, have a little holiday. What do you think?

JHANA	You going shopping?
KING	Yeah... right.
JHANA	I can shop. Okay?
KING	Why don't you stay here and get the ball rolling. I'm going to make you blueberry pancakes but I have to walk a long ways to find those berries. Maybe they're down a ravine, covered in ice. Okay? Bye, bye Jhani. You're my girl.
JHANA	I'm setting the table? Eggs? I can't do them.
KING	Sure you can.
JHANA	I make a mess.
KING	Sky's the limit for you. Don't forget that.

> KING *exits.* JHANA *wakes* BILL *who is sleeping on the couch.*

JHANA	*(quietly)* Helping me please Bill?
BILL	Fuck.
JHANA	Fuck, Bill. You're in there now? In sleeping? C'mon.
BILL	Quiet, Jhana.
JHANA	*(tries to lie on top of* BILL*)* Mum's in this. See? All tired on Daddy. He's gone. Shopping for me. We need help. You and me.
BILL	Lay off, Jhana.

JHANA   Lay off, Bill. We're like this. We're here.

BILL   What time is it?

JHANA   Cracking the eggs for Daddy. For Dad.

BILL   *(tries to sit up)* Oh God! Do I look the way I always look? Is the right side of my head caved in?

JHANA   I'll be kissing you *(kisses* BILL*)* better.

BILL   None of that.

JHANA   Andrew's funny, right?

BILL   He's a scream.

JHANA   I'll be kissing you now. *(tries to kiss* BILL *again)*

BILL   *(sitting up quickly)* Careful. There's one way to kiss certain men in the world and another way to kiss all the Bills. Most women know that instinctively.

JHANA   Dad's making pancakes and we're helping. Setting the table. Cracking the eggs. Eggs. Can you do that? The eggs. They're broken. Right?

BILL   I can crack eggs. If you stop talking I'll crack a hundred eggs.

JHANA   It's hard.

BILL   Sure is.

JHANA   Dad's asking for the eggs.

BILL	He's not asking right now. We'll deal with that when it happens.
JHANA	No. He's asking. Bill?
BILL	WHAT!
JHANA	I can't do it. I can't do the eggs.
BILL	Let's go through this. Your dear mother is sleeping happily. The King of Rock n' Roll has gone shopping. Good old Bill, who has the worst hangover ever, is supposed to give lesson on cracking the goddamned eggs.
JHANA	Good old Bill!
BILL	God in heaven.

MADDIE *enters.*

MADDIE	*(to* JHANA) Hi honey. *(to* BILL) You look awful.
JHANA	Good old Bill!
BILL	Aren't you two supposed to be at work?
MADDIE	We have a meeting with Jhana's social worker.
BILL	I thought that was Thursday.
MADDIE	That's the assessment at work, not to be confused with next week's meeting with her new one-to-one worker. But today is with Ben at eleven. Remember?
JHANA	Remember?

MADDIE	You say bye to your Dad?
JHANA	He's shopping. Pancakes, Mum.
MADDIE	I don't think so.
JHANA	With blueberries. Eggs by Bill with me in helping.
MADDIE	He didn't say goodbye?
JHANA	He's making her breakfast.
MADDIE	I don't know, Jhana. I think he's gone.
JHANA	He's shopping!
MADDIE	I think his bus went about ten minutes ago.
JHANA	Liar. He said.
BILL	*(to* MADDIE) Why don't you look horrible?
JHANA	He's shopping, Bill. For me.
BILL	I know, Jhana. I know all about it.
MADDIE	King always has a beer when he's hung over. First thing in the morning even.
BILL	And he takes the cap off with his teeth.
MADDIE	Belt buckle. Jhana? I'm pretty sure he's gone. We can wait another couple of minutes. But don't get hopeful. He's just lousy at goodbyes.
BILL	Apparently.

MADDIE	*(to* BILL) I don't need that kind of stuff right now.
BILL	Excuse me. Think I'll go crack open a cold one with my eye socket.

BILL *exits.*

MADDIE	Just before your Dad would head out on tour, I'd lie there all tangled up with him, needing the sound of his breath to fall asleep. Needing to feel everything beat inside him.
JHANA	Gone with Princie Mum.
MADDIE	But he was a regular Houdini. And I'd wake up to the sound of the van, revving up in the yard, this cold feeling in my gut, pissed off too that he wouldn't let me say goodbye. And he'd argue that these big deal farewells just made me sadder. Maybe that's true but it was also cheating.
JHANA	It's cheating Mum.
MADDIE	So I'd go in your room. Give Chatty Cathy the boot and I'd crawl into your bed.

BILL *enters.*

MADDIE	Hold on to my perfect little girl. *(holding* JHANA) You were so warm. To hell with that bed of mine that had suddenly become so big and icy. I've got Jhana.
JHANA	Me.
MADDIE	It just makes him upset to say goodbye.

JHANA	I can't without spilling. Dad's mad at me?
MADDIE	He loves you.
JHANA	It's making him sad? At me?
MADDIE	Not you.
JHANA	Dad's happy.
MADDIE	I don't know, Jhana. He's on the bus to Detroit.
JHANA	He's on the bus to Detroit, Bill.
MADDIE	That's the city where his next show is. Why don't you go get dressed and then we can make pancakes together.
JHANA	Okay, Bill?
BILL	I'm not hungry.

JHANA *exits.*

BILL	When my dad died we were all up at the cottage with him because we knew it was coming. After they came to take away, you know, his body, I lay down beside where he'd been and it was still warm there. This warmth was under the palm of my hand but seeping away. Then all the warmth was gone and I understood he was dead then. Boom.
MADDIE	Sorry, Willy.
BILL	That isn't the point. It was all right. There was something perfect about the whole thing, his living and dying. So I'm just wondering why you do it?

MADDIE	What?
BILL	Why you're screwing a ghost?
MADDIE	Shut up Bill.
BILL	No, really. I've been thinking about it and I think it all stems from your fear of death. Why else continue to haul your ex up out of the cobwebs?
MADDIE	This is bullshit.
BILL	No, this death thing makes sense on another level as well. Because you're also obsessed with a corpse: Elvis Presley. I consider the whole thing fascinating, Maddie. I really do. I mean I know that King has made him immortal now so that must be like lying down with Jesus or...
MADDIE	Tell me some more about lying down with someone, Bill. When was the last time for you?
BILL	The summer.
MADDIE	What year?
BILL	You met Carolyn. She's been doing a sessional out in the Maritimes. We're in touch.
MADDIE	Perfect. Touching through the mail or over the telephone. Very risky stuff.
BILL	It's tougher for poets. I mean the King of Rock and Roll: tight jeans, possibly a drunkard, depressed. Women are ecstatic about that sort of thing.

MADDIE	Come off it. Your crowd's got its groupies too. This is ridiculous.
BILL	Whoever fantasizes about poets? We're all supposed to be half-starved with tuberculosis, grey skin, not a sexual image.
MADDIE	If something hurt you last night then we should talk about that directly.
BILL	It hurt last night to see you as a groupie.
MADDIE	Jesus. I really can't believe this.
BILL	It hurt to see him with Jhana.
MADDIE	Okay. What else?
BILL	Nothing else.
MADDIE	C'mon, Bill. What's happened to your need to confess everything that's ever happened to you.
BILL	I don't do that.
MADDIE	You adore baring your soul. "Maddie this and this happened when I was in kindergarten. Maddie I peed myself once at cubs".
BILL	Okay. It's crossed my mind.
MADDIE	What has?
BILL	I don't mean to imply that I think about it constantly.
MADDIE	It.

BILL   You and me. Something more than, you know, boarder and... boardee. What are you anyway?

MADDIE   I'm your landlady. And you're my best friend.

BILL   Thank you. It's natural. Living here and all the stuff with Jhana that you'd think about it sometimes, about really getting together.

MADDIE   I don't think about it, Bill. I don't think of you that way.

BILL   Great. As I say it's barely crossed my mind. I mean it's like when I think of making it with the woman next door or with Queen Elizabeth. So much of sex is challenge it really is...

MADDIE   And I'm grateful for the way you are with Jhani. No. I feel blessed in that department. I really do. And with our friendship...

BILL   So you think of me as a what? Talking cocker spaniel? That sort of thing?

MADDIE   Please stop it, Bill.

BILL   I should feel encouraged. If you could fall in love with King you could fall in love with a gas station. But it makes me bored. This lack of challenge. The whole thing's remarkable. It really is.

KING   *(offstage, singing)* Since my baby left me...

BILL   Give me a break...

KING   I found a new place to dwell,
                    it's down at the end of lonely street
                    in heartbreak hotel...

                    *KING enters carrying a large bag of
                    groceries. JHANA enters.*

JHANA   My Daddy say Dad.

KING   Who's hungry?

JHANA   Me!

KING   *(sorting through bag)* Genuine one hundred
                    percent artificial maple syrup. And just for
                    you... *(handing* JHANA *a box of berries)*

JHANA   Blueberries!

KING   Through wind and rain, battles, blight, the
                    frozen-food section of the 7-11. For you my
                    love: blueberries.

JHANA   See Mum? Daddy's here! Dad.

MADDIE   He sure is. Your Dad's full of surprises.

KING   *(to* JHANA*)* How about going and opening
                    this box. Then sticking those berries in a
                    bowl.

JHANA   Put them in a bowl Bill.

MADDIE   Your Dad asked you to do it Jhana.

BILL   I'll help.

                    BILL and JHANA exit.

KING	This blues act in Detroit, she's gonna run another week. I've been put on hold.
MADDIE	And?
KING	I thought it might be nice for Jhana, not to mention the best break you've had this decade.
MADDIE	What?
KING	If I stayed on here. Just for one week.
MADDIE	Then you'd leave.
KING	Run out on the wife and kid all over again. Look, Madelaine, if you don't want me here, just say the word.
MADDIE	When you played Oshawa and had dinner here twice in a row, she thought that meant we were, you know, together again. She'll get too attached to you. Jhana will. Just like before. It's dangerous.
KING	Last night was dangerous. And very sweet.
MADDIE	She's very needy right now.
KING	How's her mother?
MADDIE	Solid as a rock. Always.
KING	I'll get my stuff.
MADDIE	*(pause)* Don't. Don't leave.
KING	Sure? Don't you want to check it out with Robert Young in there?

MADDIE   Bill!

BILL   *(off)* What?

MADDIE   King's gonna stay with us a few days. Okay?

BILL   It's your house.

KING   "A house boiled in water and blessed by no one."

          BILL *enters.*

BILL   Pardon me?

KING   "A house boiled in water and blessed by no one."

BILL   You read my book.

KING   First thing this morning. Marched up and down the "Path of Despair". Cover to cover.

BILL   Why do you remember that line? Why that one in particular?

KING   You repeated it two hundred times.

MADDIE   You want to go tell your daughter the good news?

BILL   It's like a chorus or refrain. The repeating wasn't an arbitrary decision...

KING   I liked your stuff, Bill. I'm not saying I understand it, but it sure has its moments.

BILL   Don't worry about not understanding. I feel quite strongly about that...

KING   Man you would've loved the King...

BILL   Poetry is functioning at its best when nobody
              has a clue what's going on.

              Black.

Act Two, Scene Two

                                BILL *is practicing out loud for his poetry reading and lecture.*

BILL   Fellow poets and friends. "Black Morning" has been described by critics, or critic as the case may be, as a breakthrough sequence. But breaking through into what you may well ask. *(pause)* Fuck it. *(in a Memphis accent)* I chased every woman I ever met. Know why? "Black Morning" plunges into a territory *(beat)* better left unexplored. Right. *(Memphis accent)* "Every woman adores a fascist, the boot in the face, the brute brute heart of a brute like you..." I never stopped cruising. "Black Morning" plunges into and exposes the dark underbelly of that demon called...

JHANA   *(off)* Bill!

                                  JHANA *enters, from work, very wired.*

BILL   Hi angel.

JHANA   I'm with the table. In the workshop, right?
               Fat Steffie too. She's mad. She's mad like
               this *(shakes hand violently)* Screws go
               flying, they just fly!

BILL   Steffie has a hard time controlling her
               muscles....

JHANA   She can't do it...

BILL   Maybe they've changed her medication...

JHANA   She's not on the job!

BILL   Somedays she's a real whirlwind. Right?

JHANA   A whirlwind Bill! You can't sing at work. I
               said DON'T.

BILL   Remember how you had a hard time counting
               how many screws to put in one bag? For
               Steffie —

JHANA   Steffie can't...

BILL   ...picking something up —

JHANA   Steffie...

BILL   ...is way harder than counting. And putting
               it in a little bag? It's murder.

JHANA   She can't help it, Bill.

BILL   That's right.

JHANA　　She's mad! Hitting at Peter. Mean too.
Peter can't get out of his chair. You're
scared. Right? I push Peter for lunch.
Don't walk, Bill. Peter can't. Listen to him,
(groan) he talks hard. Like hurting. It
doesn't. I'm not Peter, Bill. You're sad? At
Peter?

BILL　　A little bit.

JHANA　　Betty died.

BILL　　I remember.

JHANA　　She's not at the workshop. People die, Bill.
Dogs, television. Steffie's funny too. I'm
not scared. *(pause)* Where's my Daddy say
Dad.

BILL　　I don't know.

JHANA　　DAD!

BILL　　He's not home, Jhana. Why don't you slow
down, kick your shoes off in front of the TV.
Relax.

JHANA　　RELAX! They're new. New and just coming
in — all the little tiny screws. I'm behind
Bill. That lady's yelling on me, PAY
ATTENTION!

BILL　　I could follow you a lot better if you'd slow
down —

JHANA　　*(stomping feet in time with yelling)* PAY
ATTENTION! PAY ATTENTION! PAY
ATTENTION! PAY ATTENTION! PAY
ATTENTION... *(long pause as* JHANA
notices BILL *isn't going to pay attention,
then softly)* Hi, Billy. Be Andrew yelling
too. Bill please? Be Andrew.

BILL

Not now, Jhani. They've asked me to do a reading then a little talk on my process and that. Want to hear some?

JHANA

No. I will keep talking. See? I can sing at lunch. Not at the worktable. That worktable's for working. Everyone watches me. They love this.

BILL

What do you sing?

JHANA

(imitating Elvis) Good evening ladies and... ladies. It's pleasure. Elvis Presley is here! *(singing)* Love her tender, love her tender Never let her... Love her tender, lover her tender Love her, love her tender...

Are you watching me?

BILL

The world is watching you.

JHANA

Good. Be Andrew. For dinner, Bill. Please?

BILL

For ten minutes. When both hands are at six then you're going to be the audience and I'm going to be the brilliant young poet behind the podium. Got that?

JHANA

Yes! Get out! Out the door, Bill.

BILL *exits then* JHANA *greets him at the door, role playing a dinner date.*

JHANA

Hello Andrew.

BILL   Good evening Miss Kelly...

JHANA   She's Jhana!

BILL   You look lovely.

JHANA   Please eat.

BILL   Don't you want to take my coat first, offer me a place to sit down?

JHANA   Please sit and take your coat.

BILL   How was your day?

JHANA   Funny.

BILL   Why?

JHANA   Steffie hit Peter in the wheelchair! Screws went flying!

BILL   That doesn't sound funny.

JHANA   It's funny. Eat.

BILL   What's for dinner?

JHANA   Cheerios.

BILL   Since when do you eat Cheerios for supper.

JHANA   Since I'm funny.

BILL   Aren't you though. Are you going to make a move? Casually slip an arm around *(puts his arm around* JHANA*)* Andrew's mammoth but trembling shoulders?

JHANA
(beginning to act very sexually but toward herself not BILL) I'm funny.

BILL
You going to get in there and give Andrew the business.

JHANA
The business.

BILL
You can, Jhana. If you want to, you're allowed. You do understand that don't you?

JHANA
Kissing him on the mouth?

BILL
Absolutely. And here too. *(touching* JHANA's *neck)* I'm not saying you should rush in there and jump on him. Take it slow and easy. But you can reach out.

JHANA
Reach!

BILL
If you hold back everything it'll turn sour inside, or worse yet it'll turn into poetry. Then you're really sunk.

JHANA
Kiss his mouth, Bill.

BILL
Not me. That's your job.

JHANA
My job. And here. *(touching* BILL's *neck)* It's funny. Right? Steffie won't kiss Andrew. Only me.

MADDIE *enters.*

MADDIE
(to JHANA) Hi honey!

JHANA
NO!

MADDIE
Nice to see you too. How was your day?

JHANA   She's not allowed Bill!

BILL   We were just...

MADDIE   What am I not allowed to do?

JHANA   Get out!

MADDIE   My house kid.

JHANA   We're in private, me and Bill.

BILL   Jhana likes this guy at work and...

JHANA   NO! Make her get out!

MADDIE   Look. You're allowed to talk to Bill on your
               own but there are polite ways to explain that
               you're in the middle of something.

JHANA   Get out.

BILL   In fact it's more like pretend dates than just
               talk or...

JHANA   NO!

MADDIE   Have I interrupted you?

JHANA   NO! *(pause)* Yes.

MADDIE   You were talking about someone and my
               coming in made you embarrassed?

JHANA   We're private, me and Bill.

MADDIE   That isn't what I object to. When I come in,
               you and Bill can move upstairs after you say
               hi. No one likes being yelled at the second
               they come in the door.

JHANA   *(pause)* Sorry, Mum.

MADDIE   It's okay. How was your day?

JHANA   Hi, Mum.

MADDIE   Hi, Jhani.

JHANA   Hi, Bill.

BILL   Hi.

JHANA   How are you, Mum?

MADDIE   Fine.

JHANA   Bill is fine.

BILL   Top notch.

MADDIE   Your reading! Was that today? Jesus, Bill I meant to...

BILL   It's tomorrow. No big deal.

MADDIE   You're not nervous?

BILL   I've done dozens of these things. Or at least a certain number.

MADDIE   You need an audience?

BILL   God yes. This is a poetry reading — no one will come. And it's in a library, in Pickering.

MADDIE   I meant do you want an audience right now. To practice.

BILL   That's stupid.

MADDIE	I don't mind. Me and Jhana will be the public at large.
JHANA	I'm cooking salad.
MADDIE	Right you are! Jhana makes salad tonight! Jhana makes dessert! How many?
JHANA	Five cup!
MADDIE	One cup of... come on Jhani... oranges...
JHANA	Oranges!
MADDIE	And?
JHANA	Marshmallows. Tiny, tiny.
MADDIE	One cup...
JHANA	Coconuts... pineapple...
MADDIE	And last but not least!
JHANA	Yes!
MADDIE	What's the white stuff that holds it all together?
JHANA	Milk!
MADDIE	Sour cream!
JHANA	Sour cream!
BILL	Hallelujah!
MADDIE	Five cup salad! No recipe needed. No fuss, no muss...

JHANA   Five cup salad!

MADDIE   You know where everything is?

JHANA   The fridge. And cans.

MADDIE   And the coconut is in the cupboard above the sink in a red bag.

JHANA   Red.

MADDIE   The measuring cup is in the dishwasher. You can do all of it by yourself.

JHANA   Don't help her, Bill.

BILL   Best of luck, Jhana. And remember kid. No matter what happens in there, I loved you.

JHANA   I love you, Bill. And coconut, in a red bag, in the sink.

MADDIE   Above the sink.

JHANA   I love you, Mum.

MADDIE   Me too. Get to work.

JHANA   You're loving Bill?

MADDIE   Yup.

JHANA   She's going to work. I am working for salad and dessert.

MADDIE   And Bill and I are going to have a gigantic glass of scotch and talk poetry.

JHANA   Poetry! *(exits)*

MADDIE	So Jhana wants to sleep with someone at work?
BILL	What happened to her right to privacy?
MADDIE	I changed my mind.
BILL	Just a crush. Lots of talk about kissing.
MADDIE	"Black Morning."
BILL	Right. I'm going to use that quote about my being a voice for women and the responsibility that entails.
MADDIE	Your own voice, Bill. That's all we need.
BILL	It is my voice. Maybe I don't know how to make it sing or shimmy but it is mine.
MADDIE	However sleazy it may seem to you, I need him like breath right now.
BILL	It's your life.
MADDIE	And you're a big part of it. You're my best friend. It's true. Quit taking it like a slap in the face. You're just... I'm... I know he's fucked up. But at least he's out there. Trying to do something he feels about. He's always been, you know, very alive.
BILL	I find it remarkable that someone who makes his living pretending to be a dead person is living life to the fullest. Where is he anyway?
MADDIE	He's at the Elvis Museum in Niagara Falls. He might do some stuff for them for the anniversary in August.

BILL   What anniversary?

MADDIE   Elvis's death. Jesus, Bill. I can't believe you wouldn't know that.

BILL   It wasn't like Kennedy. I can't tell you what I was doing at that exact moment.

MADDIE   We were in Whitehorse. This guy called Wade, he came in with the news after the first set. The King is dead.

BILL   When Elvis Presley died I was at Carleton. We thought it was funny.

MADDIE   King hauled Jhana up on stage. Those days I put all my energy into convincing everyone she was normal. A little slow. Jesus. She had a ten-word vocabulary at five. Her first word was Mum and her second word was pig. Because of this story King had made up about this pig that was a terrific swimmer. But I used to worry about it anyway, mother then pig.

BILL   I bet you worried.

MADDIE   While she's up on stage I'm praying she won't open her mouth, won't stim out because of the lights, have a rocking fit because of the drums.

BILL   What'd she do?

MADDIE   Nothing. She loved it. Everyone loved her and were too pissed to notice she wasn't, you know, normal. *(pause)* Bill promise me this guy at work or some old lech on the bus isn't going to hurt her. Isn't going to take advantage of all that trust.

BILL   She's okay.

MADDIE   Mother then pig.

BILL   I think you are very wonderful with her.

MADDIE   You too, Willy.

BILL   And I have been a bit of an asshole about him staying here. A little bit.

> JHANA *enters, much slowed down, nearly dreamy.*

JHANA   It's perfect Mum. Cooking in the bowl. It's so pretty. Five cup salad. In the fridge.

MADDIE   You're all done?

JHANA   Done.

MADDIE   No problems?

JHANA   Maybe.

MADDIE   Let's not worry about it now. Come give your old Mum a hug.

JHANA   Old Mum. Old, old Mum.

MADDIE   Thanks a lot kid.

JHANA   Mine.

Black.

Act Two, Scene Three

The spot is up on KING *at the microphone, costumed like Elvis, using the Memphis accent.*

KING   I don't do any requests. Used to be I'd play whatever you asked for but I am now sick to death of everyone wanting what is bad for them, myself included. This also ties into the way I feel about women. I chased every dream going, man. They've run me ragged. All of you have.

Listen to me. It's Louisiana Hayride, 1954. Something good is happening *(touching chest)* inside here. When I sing, play guitar, you're with me. Swaying in time, singing along, you know every single word. But what's this now? Something is coming undone inside you. This is not what I mean to do. This also ties into the way I feel about women. All of them wanting to come undone. This is a very sad business and should not be part of the entertainment industry. I am just an entertainer and hold no opinions, political or otherwise. I am also, and get this clear, nobody's path of despair. Alright?

KING   Listen. *(singing)* Are you lonesome
tonight?
Do you miss me tonight?

Basically I think all of that is a load of shit.
I sing that sort of thing fourteen times a
night, on stage or rocking inside the arms of
some woman. You wanna know the truth
man? Everytime I sing it, I believe the whole
thing entirely. Like I keep saying, I don't
take requests.

Black.

Act Two, Scene Four

—————————————————————————————————

> MADDIE *and* JHANA *are going through*
> JHANA's *report from the workshop.*

MADDIE

The top part says they're recommending you do another term at the workshop, that advancement seems premature. In other words, you screwed up and aren't going anywhere. The bottom part breaks everything down and explains why — poor attitude, inconsistent work habits, frequenting washroom as much as ten times in a single morning, distracting other workers... What are you doing in the bathroom all day?

> KING *enters.*

JHANA

Nothing.

MADDIE

I asked you a question. What are you doing in the bathroom all day?

JHANA

Periods. You're sore in your stomach Mum. Twice.

KING

Maybe I shouldn't be here.

MADDIE

This is exactly when you should be here. If you have cramps you take a blue pill.

JHANA   A football.

MADDIE   A blue pill shaped like a football.

JHANA   They're in her purse?

MADDIE   What are you doing in the bathroom all day?

JHANA   What are you doing in the bathroom all day?

KING   Maybe she doesn't understand the question Maddie.

MADDIE   This isn't a joke, Jhana. Are you in there by yourself?

JHANA   Maybe.

MADDIE   This is a job. An honest-to-God grown up job. You're not a little school girl or...

JHANA   You're not allowed.

MADDIE   I know you're not. You're not allowed to slack off or spend the day sitting on the lid of the toilet.

JHANA   You! You're not allowed to know. Bill said.

KING   What's he got to do with this?

JHANA   I'm trying! Counting four, opening the bags...

MADDIE   What are you going to do if you don't make it at the workshop, Jhana? Have you thought about that?

JHANA   Yes.

MADDIE	Good. Fill me in. What are you going to do for a living?
JHANA	So? I don't care.
MADDIE	What's the big plan?
JHANA	*(hugging* KING) Helping Daddy. Helping Dad.
MADDIE	How is it you're going to help? Carry his guitar?
JHANA	Okay.
MADDIE	Stay up all night with the roadies and sleep until noon?
KING	Madelaine...
JHANA	Okay!
MADDIE	Jesus, Jhani.
JHANA	I'm singing! See? I'm singing beside Daddy.
MADDIE	Good Christ.
JHANA	*(sung)* Love her tender, love her tender...
MADDIE	ME tender. ME! You don't know the right words. And you have to sing the whole song right through. Those are things you can't do. Those things aren't possible for you.
JHANA	Love HER ME tender. ME!

MADDIE	What do you think King? Has she got the job?
KING	Come on Maddie. Get off her back.
JHANA	Andrew likes it. Andrew loves my singing.
MADDIE	Andrew is very disappointed in you right now.
JHANA	He loves me.
MADDIE	He's given you one chance after another this month. If he wasn't so new at it he wouldn't be anywhere near this patient.
JHANA	Andrew loves me.
MADDIE	Andrew is your boss.
JHANA	He's my boyfriend.
MADDIE	He's your supervisor. Quit the nonsense.
JHANA	He loves me.
MADDIE	He is someone that you work for. It has nothing to do with boyfriends or any of that. It has to do with you screwing up at work.
JHANA	Shut up! Make her shut up!
MADDIE	And you're following him around all day. Why are you doing that?
JHANA	He hates you Mum! Andrew hates you!
MADDIE	Sitting in his car. Is that true?

JHANA	Andrew hates you! And Daddy! Daddy hates you! And me! Hate you, hate you!
MADDIE	Go up to your room until you cool down. Until you can talk decently.
JHANA	You're going to the workshop! You're hating it more and you're not allowed Mum. Nobody's allowed. *(picking up coat and heading for the door)*
MADDIE	Where do you think you're going?
JHANA	Where do you think you're going? You Mum!
MADDIE	I want you back in here and...
JHANA	YOU MUM! YOU'RE NOT ALLOWED!

JHANA *exits out front door.*

MADDIE	You know how when she's mad she sort of goose steps but keeps her head down low? I'll bet she's doing that now. Curtains are parting. Someone's saying it's that girl out there. What do they call her? Probably just retarded.
KING	Special. Isn't that the latest?
MADDIE	Naw, just social workers say that, teachers.
KING	Well that accounts for half the neighbourhood.
MADDIE	Simple. People still say that I'll bet.

KING   People aren't that out of it, Maddie.
              Everyone has a cousin or someone who is....

MADDIE   Not everyone has a daughter.

KING   Hey. She's mine too. My family. My little
              girl.

MADDIE   Do you think I'm too awful to her? I should
              go out there. She's probably ripping up the
              neighbour's lawn or something. Taking off
              like this? That's something she just started
              this year because she know it makes me crazy.

KING   She's okay. Just let her cool off.

MADDIE   When I was a kid there was a boy that lived
              near us in this orange house. I think he had
              Cerebral Palsy but really handicapped. Even
              their house looked different. The colour
              seemed too bright. You know how when you
              go away for a while then when you come
              back everything looks different? Their house
              looked like that all the time. Sort of charged
              up but dead all at once.

KING   Slow down now, Madelaine.

MADDIE   This is my house. People look at my house
              that way...

KING   Always so hard on yourself.

MADDIE   My home. I was shitty to her just now. I've
              got to find her.

KING   Talk to me. Tell me about your day and...

MADDIE

That guy died didn't he? Wade. Remember the guy who sang Elvis all night up in Whitehorse?

KING

Hit by a truck.

MADDIE

Jhana's great in traffic. It took forever to learn but even on the side streets, not a car around for miles. She's checking it out thoroughly from the curb, looking both ways... I'm going to find her.

KING

You walked her to school until she was fifteen. It's not right, your hanging on like that.

MADDIE

And now she's eighteen and I want to hold on more than ever, protect her from all of them. You bet.

KING

You think everyone is some kind of rapist?

MADDIE

I think it's worse than that. I think everyone out there thinks Jhana's doing just fine.

KING

Weren't you going to get her in a group home?

MADDIE

You're as bad as the rest.

KING

So Jhana's gonna live with you until you're both old and gray. Great Madelaine, you two seem to get along real well.

MADDIE

Her name's on a list for supervised apartments. Okay?

> MADDIE *tries to leave, but* KING *keeps her back.*

KING   No. Not okay.

MADDIE   Don't tell me —

KING   She's mine too —

MADDIE   Part time. Between shows and women and —

KING   Look. I'm not here to fight with anyone.

MADDIE   Then you deal with her. You get her keyed up to make lunch, go to the workshop, do up her buttons right, keep her hair clean, her hands off the men on the bus...

KING   I ask how your day is and you tell me about her.

MADDIE   What time is it?

KING   It's like you've disappeared.

MADDIE   What is it you want from me? I don't know why you stayed on this week if it was just to —

KING   I want to come home.

MADDIE   Yeah right. Then you get to leave again.

KING   I'm talking about staying. Leaving is not part of the picture.

MADDIE   You sure?

KING   No. Let her go stomping around and make the whole fucking neighbourhood crazy.

MADDIE   I get scared there isn't anything left inside
                that's just me.

KING   Bring me home Maddie.

MADDIE   I don't even know how to remember things
                that are all mine. That happened before she
                was born. Did it change you that way?

KING   I guess so.

MADDIE   Right inside? That happened to you too?

KING   I don't know. I don't examine it all to death
                the way you do. The way she is has nothing
                to do with you.

MADDIE   We made her life —

KING   It has to do with oxygen being cut off at
                birth. That has nothing to do with either of
                us.

MADDIE   How can that be true...

KING   Don't do this.

MADDIE   If I could've held her inside longer, maybe
                she'd have been stronger —

KING   We've been over this a thousand times. It
                doesn't make sense to keep —

MADDIE   Nobody King, is ever allowed to talk to me
                about what makes sense.

                Black.

Act Two, Scene Five

JHANA   She killed me.

BILL   Who did?

JHANA   Mum killed me.

BILL   If your mum killed you, you wouldn't be here to tell me about it. You'd be dead.

JHANA   Princie's dead.

BILL   But not Jhana. You just got in trouble last night for riding around for three hours on the Woodbine bus.

JHANA   It's funny, right?

BILL   Not really. And talking to people you don't know about your troubles isn't such a great idea either. The bus driver that phoned last night...

JHANA   I hate him.

BILL   He was a nice guy, Jhani. He got worried. We all did.

JHANA   Be Andrew please. Be Andrew.

BILL   You have to change your thinking about Andrew. I didn't realize he was, you know, *(beat)* your boss.

JHANA   Good evening Andrew and —

BILL   Rule Number One: Don't get hung up on the
                boss. Rule Number Two: Don't fall for any
                guy who *(pause)* doesn't see the world in the
                same way you do. Right? You had breakfast
                yet? I'm starving.

JHANA   Starving. I'm pretty, Bill.

BILL   Yes you are. How about Smitty's. Then
                maybe we can go along the Danforth and
                look for something for your mum. Sort of
                make up for last night.

JHANA   He likes me.

BILL   We can take the subway.

JHANA   Andrew likes me and drying my face.

BILL   I don't doubt that for a minute but he
                doesn't like to see you outside work or any of
                that. It isn't possible. You ever tried kissing
                your elbow? *(demonstrates)* Can't be done.
                No matter how hard you try. It's impossible.

JHANA   Liar Bill. Steffie's hitting and Peter can't get
                out of his chair. *(pause)* Andrew loves me.

BILL   Look. These are the rules and they stink.

JHANA   Stink.

BILL   Fall in love with someone you work with or
                someone from your school —

JHANA   No! No one likes you, Bill. No, no, no, no.
                No one. You said I'll be kissing, I'll be
                phoning Andrew...

BILL   I made a mistake. Okay? Look, Steffie
            believes that Barry Manilow is going to ask
            her on a date. And everyone loves teasing
            Steffie about that. But at the same time you
            know Barry Manilow isn't really going to take
            Steffie out anywhere. It's sort of like that
            with you and Andrew or you and the guy
            next door, the man on the bus. It isn't really
            going to happen. So you just stick to the
            guys from your own turf. With Rory or
            Jason or those brothers with the big heads.

JHANA   I am loving Andrew. Loving him now and
            you said. *(pause)* Pig.

BILL   You got it, Jhana. Lots of those around but
            I didn't invent any of it. In my world Barry
            Manilow would have to do time putting
            screws in a bag and you and Steffie would be
            on stage at Maple Leaf Gardens.

JHANA   Bill?

BILL   You'd sing, strut, tell your story. Everyone
            seeing you live for the first time.

JHANA   I want a boyfriend.

BILL   I still think that can happen.

JHANA   Be Andrew. Please be Andrew.

BILL   You be Jhana and I'll be Bill.

JHANA   Good evening and... Bill? Are you sad?

BILL   Yes.

JHANA   At me? Be mad at me, don't.

BILL	You are my favourite girl in the whole world. *(placing arms around* JHANA*)* Did you know that? C'mon. Go put on something fancy. I'm taking you to Smitty's for breakfast.
JHANA	Kiss, kiss, kiss, kiss, kiss. Kiss her mouth, Bill.
BILL	Naw, friends don't do that. They keep clear of that sort of thing.
JHANA	Do it tiny. Once.

BILL *kisses* JHANA's *cheek.*

JHANA	Do it tiny again. Kiss her mouth, Bill. Kiss her bigger.

BILL *looks closely at* JHANA, *he turns her face toward him, holds her face for a long time then kisses her, long and full on the mouth.* KING *appears on the stairs.*

JHANA	Bigger.
BILL	I can't sweetheart.
KING	Don't move.
JHANA	My Daddy say Dad.
KING	*(coming downstairs)* Stand up, Jhani. Get away from that couch. *(to* BILL*)* Get out.
JHANA	Why?
KING	*(to* JHANA*)* Go upstairs.

JHANA   Going to Smitty's me and Bill.

KING   *(to* BILL) Get out.

BILL   It isn't like that...

KING   Get the fuck out!

BILL   I was just...

JHANA   You can come Dad. Gone to Smitty's...

KING   Jhana shut up.

JHANA   Jhana shut up.

KING   Don't you ever come near my daughter again.

BILL   This is my house too...

JHANA   You're kissing Bill?

KING   *(to* JHANA) Get up those stairs!

BILL   I'll go up your goddamned stairs.

JHANA   I'll go up your goddamned stairs.

BILL   Hey Maddie!

JHANA   Hey Maddie!

BILL   *(heading up stairs)* I'm being evicted by a dead pop singer.

MADDIE *enters.*

KING   You're pushing it man.

BILL   I've seen you. With both of them. You
                never get in close enough to be pushed.

MADDIE   What's going on?

KING   He was all over Jhana.

MADDIE   Are you okay?

JHANA   We don't tell people to shut up around here.

MADDIE   What happened?

KING   He's been feeling her up.

MADDIE   I don't believe that.

BILL   Fuck you.

KING   I'm warning you man...

JHANA   Shut up, shut up!

                BILL *heads for door.*

JHANA   Can I come?

BILL   This house is too small —

JHANA   I'm small!

KING   You said it.

JHANA   I'll be smaller. See?

MADDIE   Look if everyone would just —

JHANA   Look at me!

BILL   Now the two of you can go drive to Jesus. Just like the good old days in Moosebone, Alberta.

MADDIE   Jesus, Bill. I just spent half the night lecturing Jhana on running away when she's pissed off —

JHANA   *(crouching down)* I'm small now!

KING   Maybe you didn't hear me Madelaine. He was all over Jhana when I came down.

BILL   You don't even know who Jhana is.

         KING *knocks* BILL *down to the floor.*

JHANA   *(running to* BILL) Bill! Up Bill! Get up!

BILL   I can't just yet.

MADDIE   I'm sorry, Willy.

KING   Ah Christ we're all sorry. Get up.

JHANA   He's hurting. Take a blue pill, Bill. A football. In your stomach.

BILL   Thanks a lot, Jhana.

MADDIE   *(to* KING) Leave. Go pack your stuff.

KING   What?

MADDIE   You're going to do it again anyway. Let's just get it over with. I mean it King.

KING   I'm doing my best here, Maddie...

MADDIE   It isn't enough.

KING   She's my family.

MADDIE   My family is down on the floor.

JHANA   My Daddy say Dad.

KING   You just stepped over the line lady.

MADDIE   I know.

                KING *exits.*

JHANA   *(picks up phone, dials 911)* My name is
                Jhana Gladys Kelly. I am mentally
                handicapped. I live at three TWO nine
                Chisholm Avenue. I live in Toronto. Help
                me please nine one one. They are hurt.

                Black.

Epilogue

The spot on KING, *downstage, costumed like Elvis, at microphone, addressing audience in the Memphis accent.*

KING
Thank you very much ladies and gentlemen. You've been a wonderful audience. Before I go, I wanna tell you something nice about my kid. Lisa's out back of the house playing with this ratty dog of her mother's which I hate. She's trying to make this dog sit and that. She's being real bossy which sort of cracked me up because I mean she's a real little kid. The dog's antsy and being a dog. Finally it does settle down and you know what she does? She sings to him. She's pretending she's me. Even has the moves down right. I felt great. I mean someone pretending to be me but not to make fun and that. It's nice. But what's even better is that she's my kid and I just... Lord. Just a little. What I'm trying to say is she might love me.

KING *walks off stage, spot is still on microphone.* JHANA *enters in her nightgown and Elvis cape, and speaks into the microphone.*

JHANA
Hello. HELLO MAPLE LEAF GARDENS! IT'S ME! JHANA! DO YOU LIKE ME? Bill says you can't. C'mon. Try. *(trying to kiss her elbow)*

JHANA   Elvis is on the mouths of women all the time.
             She likes it. He sings "Loves ME, loves
             ME". He is happy and I love him back.
             You know on the bus? The Woodbine Bus?
             The black hair is in front of you. Don't
             touch it. You're not allowed. Princie's back
             is sunny and I'm laying my head there but
             not now. *(tries kissing elbow again)* See?
             She's this far away. *(shows distance with
             fingers)* Trying and trying. Bill says you
             can't. He kisses there for me. Steffie tries
             this too.

             No one will know and don't tell. Right? But
             I am *(arms out to audience)* kissing you.
             Now.

             Black.

             The End

JEWEL

For my family and for Aimee.

The original version of *Jewel* was performed at The Banff Centre, February, 1985. This version, revised and expanded substantially, premiered at Tarragon Theatre in Toronto, April, 1987.

MARJORIE   *Joan MacLeod*

Directed by Andy McKim.
Set and costume design by Linda Muir.
Lighting design by Heather Sherman.
Stage manager — Beth Bruck.

The Setting

The play is set in the Peace River Valley on Valentine's Day, 1985, in Marjorie's mobile home.

The Characters

Marjorie Clifford is 30 years old.

The Running Time

The play runs approximately one hour with no intermission.

Prologue

MARJORIE *is standing in her nightgown beside a full bucket of fresh milk. She speaks directly to the audience.*

MARJORIE   Valentine's through the ages. You are six years old and folding up this gigantic piece of white tissue paper until it's the size of your hand then attacking it with these dull little scissors, chopping the corners off, driving a hole right through the middle. But when you unfold it — pure magic: triangles and diamonds pinwheeling out from the centre, a thousand crescent moons. So you cut out this heart and paste it onto red cardboard. Print his name very carefully, then your own name, right along side. It's so special you can barely stand it. Only when you get to school you discover that every girl in your class has done the very same thing. And the most popular boy in the world just stuffs all those valentines into his desk without saying a word. By the end of the afternoon you realize that some of those hearts have turned into paper airplanes, some into spitballs. Valentine's through the ages. Alright.

You are thirteen and at the Claresholme Teen Stomp and everything is dumb: the red punch, the heart-shaped plates, Claresholme, the records that are all old and country. But the dumbest thing ever is Lucy who you're down here visiting.

Lucy is fifteen and what your mother calls
mature meaning she has big tits, smokes and
is also stupid. She visited you last month and
was afraid to get on an escalator. But it gets
worse. Because right now, Lucy is dancing
with some wonderful boy and she's danced
ten thousand times since she got here. You
haven't been asked once. You also don't care
a damn but there goes Lucy again, right up to
the boys lining the rear wall of the gym. She
tells them to go dance with her cousin
Marjorie. That's you. And it's like all your
nerves have gone electric and the air too.
Nobody moves. They're just lined up like
some kind of firing squad, a big string of
monkeys and now all you can look at is their
boots and the dumb floor. Lucy says please
and that you're an orphan, which isn't true,
but you still just die. No matter how many
times you tell dumb-ass Lucy she still wants
to hear about orphanages and that.

Then you notice it — black cowboy boots two
feet in front of you. And someone you're
afraid to look at is asking you to dance.
Okay. It's a slow song. You decide to kill
yourself but there you are now. You can do
it. Damp hands bumping together. His neck
is red as a brick. He speaks. "Where you
from?" And you're still afraid to look at
him but by some miracle you manage it,
"Calgary."

Then two perfect minutes, moving ever-so-
small, one side to another. You just want to
take a peek. His eyes are flat and brown as a
frozen puddle and staring straight at your
cousin Lucy. Suddenly he looks clean into
you and tells you he wouldn't live in Calgary
if it was the last place on earth. And it feels

so stupid and mean. "That's fine," you tell
him. That's just great. Then you explain
how the Beatles love Calgary and that they're
moving there next month.

Everything changes. He is looking at you
special. Some of the others are too.
Questions come from everywhere. "When?
What would they do that for? Have you met
them?" And for the first time, you, are right
at the centre of a very perfect world.
Invented, but still perfect. Valentine's
through the ages. You are thirteen years old
and dizzy with love.

Two years later, you're at a sleepover. Nine
other girls there in flannel nighties. You've
all arrived with an inch of liquor, stolen from
your folks' rye and scotch and gin bottles.

You mix this up with a twenty-sixer of Tahiti
Treat and sit cross-legged in a circle, passing
the bottle around. Everytime you take a sip,
you tell a truth — how you went to second
with so and so. Who it is you're really in
love with this week. It's all marvelous. It's
all made up. You're half-sick with pink
liquor and trying to French inhale Peter
Jackson cigarettes. You light a candle and
listen to Joni Mitchell sing *Both Sides Now*
eleven times in a row. You're delirious with
sadness. You phone up a dozen boys, say
something absolutely filthy then hang up the
phone. This liquor in your gut. This tingling
in your legs. You are fifteen years old and
sick with love.

Valentine's through the ages marches on.
You've been going to the university and are
all grown up. You have a boyfriend — this

range management student who comes from
the Arctic Circle. Well nearly. Range
management: the choreography *(beat)* of
cows. You met in February but now it's
August. You're camping near his folks' place
in northern Alberta. You're out of your
territory. *(beat)* And you love it. Because
there is something about him and this place
that's like coming home after a long, long
journey. And it's true in a way, coming
home.

The inside of your blue nylon tent sweats in
the morning sun. Through this gauzy half-
moon of a window mosquitoes crash around;
two little kids collect beer bottles in a potato
sack, eat O'Henry bars at six a.m.

The cattle arranger, with his sleeping bag
zipped up with yours, is enjoying the sleep of
the dead. You are enjoying this chance to
examine his face: high cheekbones, lashes
like a woman's, black hair sticking out in a
million directions. Out of your territory.
And last night, at six minutes to midnight, he
asked you to stay out of your territory
forever. Marriage. "Marry me, Marjorie."
There's this land he's wanting to buy and no
money for cattle yet but the oil patch is right
around the corner. He's got his welder's
papers. The money will flow. Maybe five
winters of working out then full-time farming
or ranching or whatever. He talks about
buying a milk cow and *(picking up bucket)*
you nearly pass out with the romance of it.
One of his hands is against his heart as if he
were taking a pledge. And the other one is
meandering up your nightgown. Valentine's
through the ages.

A country song starts up softly on radio.

Six years later now. You're still crazy with
love.

Scene One

Lighting change signifies that
MARJORIE *is now in her trailer. She
turns up the radio and carries her bucket
into the kitchen area. While singing
along to the radio she pours milk into
two large glass jars and places them in
the fridge. She removes another milk jar
from the fridge and skims the cream off
the top. She listens to Message Time.
She drinks beer.*

MARJORIE   Christ I'm thirsty. Thirsty for everything
except milk. Your dad made this beer. I
mean it doesn't taste terrible but it sort of
leaves fur on your teeth. No one can really
make good beer, they all just think they can,
and are dying for you to drink this flat stuff
that's clear as mud. Oh well, Harry. You
know what they say to do with failed beer?
Drink it.

RADIO   And that's it for Country Countdown
tonight. Happy Valentine's. And you better
snuggle up to the one you love because,
according to Environment Canada, it's a
chilly thirty-three below in Fort St. John
tonight and it looks like it's going to dip
down even lower.

MARJORIE   You hear that Harry? Cozy up.

RADIO   And now Message Time. The link between
              you and your loved ones. A community
              service brought to you by CKNL North
              Country.

MARJORIE   You'll have to stay quiet for a minute. Think
              you can manage that?

RADIO   To Connie Brown: Happy Valentine's. Wish
              I could be there with love from Stanley. To
              Cynthia, Ruthie and Jason; home on
              Saturday, love from your daddy, Jason
              Senior. To Beatrice George; call Credit
              Union immediately, very important.

MARJORIE   Poor Beatrice. They're broke.

RADIO   To Billy Gustafson; your cattle are out and in
              Chevron property south of Fish Creek.
              Remove at once. To Marjorie Clifford;

MARJORIE   Yes sir.

RADIO   Your order is in at Buckerfields'. Will be
              delivered on the 17th.

MARJORIE   Well it's about time.

RADIO   To Rebecca Cochrane; not coming home as
              planned, will call on Saturday, Aubrey
              Cochrane. To Sally Harper; Happy
              Valentines. You are my one and only, love
              Frank.

MARJORIE *turns off radio.*

MARJORIE   You know Harry? I was listening to Message
Time. When was it? Christmas Eve, years
ago. You were working for Esso out on
Cotcho Lake. I'd just come up from school
and missed you by half a day. I mean that
first year of being married we must've spent
all of ten minutes together. So me and Deb
are drinking egg nog and listening to the
messages. They're gushy as hell. "To Ruth
in Dawson who I met in the bar last night. I
love you more than life itself." That sort of
thing. Even Debbie got something half-way
romantic from Walter. And I'm sitting there
waiting then getting worried that maybe you
forgot. Then realizing you'd never do that
and getting very excited and it comes. "To
Marjorie Clifford. Merry Christmas. The
calf will be needing her worm shot on the
twenty-seventh." Period.

Was I pissed off Harry? I threw my egg nog
at the radio. And then I start to stand up for
you. Defend your good name. Telling
Debbie how you're really very romantic but in
a private sort of way. Which was true
enough I suppose.

*The sound of a dog barking is heard
outside.*

But Jesus. Worm shot.

No! You've been outside for all of two
seconds. Go chase a weasel. That dog,
Harry. Remember going down to
Beaverlodge to buy him? Staying in that very
lousy motel called Shady Glenn or Palm
Grove — some Prairie name like that. And

the guy with the litter's explaining that this
dog's part wolf. I mean there's no person
north of Edmonton that doesn't own a dog
part wolf. It can be purebred Chihuahua and
people round here would still say "Careful.
That dog's got wolf in it." So we buy this
thing that looks like a guinea pig and, in a fit
of inspiration, we name him *(beat)* Wolf.

And on the way home, he's sitting on the
floor of the truck, quivering for a hundred
miles. He hasn't changed. I mean he's big
now. In fact he's fat. His only goal in life
seems to be figuring out a way of never going
outside. I think Wolf would rather live with
my folks in the city, eat canned dog food,
and lie around all day on their wall-to-wall.

I meant to explain why I never came home
last night. No Harry. I was not out fooling
around. I was at Debbie's. She put the kids
to bed and we made this massive supper.
Walter had just gone back to the bush and I
guess the guy that picked him up had this bag
of shrimp, fresh from the coast that morning.
So we shucked them or whatever the hell it is
you do with shrimp. And we made this white
wine sauce. Then drank what was left over
which was about a gallon each. Deb's doing
fine. I mean her and Walter are in debt over
this new tractor like you wouldn't believe but
they're making out. Where was I? Deb's last
night — right.

So we're just sitting there talking and getting
very drunk and there's this knock at the door.
It's not even eight-thirty but feels around
midnight and I'm thinking, shit — it's your
dad. Then it dawns on me that Munroe's

never knocked on a door in his life. He just
comes in and yells, "I'm here! Where's the
coffee?"

Well. Guess who? Guess who wears sensible
shoes and overcoats and, more than likely,
have a good case of pimples on the go? It's
the Mormons.

Come all the way from the state of Utah to
bring us the word of God. I don't get up off
the couch. That is to say I'm incapable of
getting off the couch. And I'm thinking —
this is great. We actually live in a place that
needs missionaries. I mean I know they do
their business in the cities too but I'm
pretending the North is like darkest Africa
and that Deb and me have rings through our
noses and these big, black breasts hanging out
front, like torpedos, like National
Geographic. And the younger one, he's all of
eighteen or something. He asks me if I've
been saved and I tell him, "UNGOWA!"

These two are very embarrassed. They pack
up their stuff, give us some pamphlets, head
out into forty below in this little Japanese
car. We laugh about it for a while longer
then end up feeling bad. I mean it's like
being drafted, it's something they have to do.

I stayed over night. Which is something I do
quite often when Walter's off in the bush.
We sleep in the same bed and hug and that
but it's not gay or anything. It's just very
nice when you're on your own to have other
people close by. And we understand one
another quite well. Debbie and me.

*The sound of a dog barking is heard
outside.*

No! Go make some friends. That dog.
Wolf must've had something very horrible
happen to him when he was real young. Old
Wolf and me, eh? Or maybe before we got
hold of him that guy beat him, or his mother
tried to eat him. Yeah, that suits Wolf. He's
just hanging around with all his brothers and
sisters, trying to have a good time and his
mother tries to eat him.

Remember when we tried to take him hunting
for lynx? Wolf is obsessed with thoughts of
his own death and refuses to leave the truck.
Your wife, who is me, is also obsessed with
death but is equally obsessed with making this
marriage work. Lucky for you, the shits for
me. How's your beer there, Harry? You're
looking a little pale around the edges tonight.

Wanna dance? C'mon dance with me.
*(Turning on radio and dancing to fiddle
waltz.)*

It's Valentine's night at the Ranch Cabaret.
We're dancing to a band called Hot
Lightning. Dancing tight and slow. Your
shirt smelling like cedar and diesel. Smoke.

We've been ice fishing all day. The sky just
getting heavy with snow when we leave for
town, the dark coming in. By the time we get
there, these big flakes. Everything pretty as
Christmas cards.

Your folks are there. Your mother waltzing
bolt upright and scared, shy at being in town.

Your eyes in her face — that wonderful jade.
Munroe leading her, proud and near drunk.
His arm around me at the table for the first
time. Telling how when you were little you
stole his truck and sunk it in the lake. All of
us proud and near drunk. This mirror ball's
sprinkling light all round the room and across
your face. We've just gone into life-time debt
for buying the land and this trailer. I believe
we are perfectly happy. That is to say, I, am
perfectly happy.

RADIO
And that's our request waltz for this evening
and goes out to Mr. and Mrs. R. Johnson.
And now more easy listening on CKNL, your
north country station.

She turns off the radio.

MARJORIE
And on the way home in the pick-up, all four
of us squeezed inside, your dad says —
"Look at them cheeks of Marjorie's, all
glowy and red. I like that in a woman.
Looks freshly slapped." And I think, great,
I've married into a family of insane people.
But I figured it out pretty quick — this father
and son. When you went down, Munroe was
the only one that didn't mind my staying
quiet, that could keep comfortable with it.

They're still looking out for me, Harry.
They're both doing fine. *(pause)* That was
nice. You are some dancer. In fact you're
wearing me out.

Today I was at the Co-op in town, buying
groceries and that. This kid is pushing the
buggy. I think he's one of Beatrice's boys
but then it's hard to keep track. And this
other kid who's working there yells from
across the parking lot, "Hey Mitchell!

What's got four legs, is three hundred feet
tall and goes down on Newfoundland?'' And
this kid Mitchell looks real embarrassed. You
can just tell he's praying his buddy over there
will shut up. Because old Mitchell knows
who I am. I mean I am one hell of a famous
widow Harry. We're talking Time magazine.
Reporters all the way from Texas braving
forty below and gravel roads just to get a
picture of me and Wolf. And this kid yells it
again, "Mitch? What's a thousand feet tall,
has four legs and goes down on
Newfoundland?'' And I end up apologizing!
Saying I've always been one to make jokes
about anything and everything. This idiot, he
yells it out *(beat)* "The Ocean Ranger!''
(beat) Old Mitch practically has a heart
attack right on the spot. By the time he's got
the truck loaded it looks like he's decided to
be a priest.

You know I always thought it was a
ridiculous name — the Ocean Ranger. Like a
speedboat full of Girl Guides. And when you
first got the job I just panicked because I
didn't know how to imagine you there.
That's important Harry. It's important to
women who have husbands who work out to
know how to imagine them in a place. I
mean all I had to do was drive into town or
walk to your dad's to see a rig on the ground,
to set you somewhere. And usually you were
just up around Nelson and I knew that if I
really went squirrelly I could jump in the
truck and find you. But Newfoundland!
That is practically four thousand miles away.
Right from the start it felt wrong. I mean
we're supposed to be farmers and there you
are out on this floating thing in the middle of
some ocean. The Atlantic Ocean.

And when I got the call that you'd gone
down, all I could think was that you were
drifting, that you might sink for a minute,
then get caught up in kelp or some current,
and set off again, that you'd never settle.
You'd never arrive on something solid again.
And I thought about that Harry, non-stop.
Thought about that for fourteen months
without a break.

Then I'm living with my folks, and my
mother, she signs me up for some god-awful
thing called a grieving workshop. All this
group stuff going on that just makes me
mental. I mean this is a very private business
if you ask me. Everyone wanting me to come
to terms with this. Those sort of expressions
are another thing that makes me crazy.
They're just pieces of air. And all I'm really
wanting is for everyone just to leave me
alone. Some church ran this thing and
they're tossing scripture around like a volley
ball. I mean as if that's going to fill my bed
or help me make payments.

Okay, we got our money since then. But I
mean this isn't some cheque that just showed
up in the mail one day. This is after two
years of drawn out bull shit with lawyers and
Louisiana accents. Every time you open the
paper or a magazine or letter, more stuff
about the Ocean Ranger. What I want,
through the whole inquiry, is to narrow it
down to one man. But we couldn't even
narrow it down to one company. But it's still
what I keep wanting, just pare it all down.
Leave me one man, up there on the top floor,
behind some marble top desk.

I want him to say "Yup, I'm your boy, it was
my fault. My fault about the design flaws,
the lack of survival suits, my fault about the
evacuation procedure and that the lifeboats
would've gone down in a lake. I'm your boy.
Not that I meant any of it but I sure as hell
did screw things up. You think safety is top
priority but it gets lost somewhere along the
way. You get tested like that and completely
fail the test. I screwed up. Big time".

I don't want to cause this man any harm.
But I would like to place him aboard a
drilling platform, after midnight in February,
over a hundred miles from the coast of
Newfoundland. An alarm calls this man
from sleep and onto a deck that is pitch black
and tipped over fifteen degrees and all
covered in ice. The wind is screaming. Salt
water and snow pelt his face. Everybody is
running around and nobody knows what to
do. He is in his pajamas and being lowered
in a life raft with twenty other men, into a
sea of fifty foot waves.

Then I would reach down and lift that man
up from this terrible place just like the hand
of God come to save him. Remove him from
all that terror and certain death. I place him
somewhere warm and dry. Relief here and
family. Take his shivering hand inside my
own and turn his hand over and over and
over. Until he sees it. Palm up and attached
and staring straight at him. His hand is the
hand of God and he could have gathered
them all up. Saved eighty-four men from the
North Atlantic. He chose not to.

And I don't care who owns you mister. I
don't care if you're ODECO or Mobil Oil, a
fed or provincial. My sadness, my husband's
death — it was handmade by someone.

You know at first, right after, I thought my
insides were made out of paper. Very white
paper. I would even walk carefully because I
thought something might rip inside. Where
am I? Right. We were talking about the
grieving workshop. I go off in a corner with
a Bible just so they won't bug me. And I
actually found something that made sense:
the book of Genesis, page one, "Let the
waters teem with living creatures and let the
birds fly above the earth within the vault of
Heaven. And so it was, God created great
whales."

Well. I hold onto those lines like a goddamn
life jacket. I start pretending you are this
very fine whale with the sun on your back
and just having the life of Riley in general.

You see, Harry. What I loved about that is
I'm thinking you have no heart and no
memory. I mean I know that whales have
warm blood and a heart and that but it's not
the sort that makes you barge through
everything like some open nerve. And I
thought, that's the ticket. No heart and no
memory. I thought that was about the best
way to live that anyone had ever come up
with.

Very crazy stuff. Well old friend. *(looking
at ring)* You don't have a heart and you
don't have a memory anymore. I suppose
that part's the truth. But I do.

Even this summer. I'd just moved back here and everyone was so worried that I'd go crazy again. And sure enough, that's when I started having these little night-time chats of ours. But it wasn't like now.

I'd tell you about the kid driving grain truck, the one helping out with harvest. I'd bring him out these sandwiches at noon. Because of the heat, he would take off his shirt and this line of sweat would sort of weep down his belly. We lean against the wheel of the truck for shade and drink ice water out of a thermos, passing it back and forth.

And I told you I took him to the granary. The air is very cool in there. We take off all our clothes without looking at one another. He folds up his jeans and makes a pillow, like for under my head. The floor boards and loose seed cut into the backs of my legs. Everything smells very clean and very dry. Like gravel. And I mean this kid is really inside. And he's moving above me and on me and all around me. And it's like there are these thousands of minnows that have just been sleeping under my skin forever and all at once they rush for the surface. And it's... it's, *(beat)* bravery. And I think, fuck you, Harry! Dying and leaving me is about the most gutless thing anyone could ever do.

All those stories about that kid driving grain truck? I made everyone of them up. Just wanting to make you jealous. Just trying to make you mad. Trying every trick in the book to get some kind of response. I mean he was barely seventeen or something That's called the Angry Phase, Harry. I think I'm starting to come out of it though.

I'll tell you a story that's true. There is a guy
teaching school here that I've gone out with a
few times. Some dinners in town. Last week
we went to a play in Dawson Creek. He's a
very nice man. Sort of shy. Or maybe it's
lack of character. No. There's something
quite good there.

He comes from Vancouver which is kind of
an excuse but you know what he reminds me
of? Me. When I first got here. All set to
live on roots and berries, grow our own
vegetables and animals and furniture. Seeing
your folks' place for the first time I
remember thinking — this is great — big old
log house, smoke in the chimney. Your
mum's real warm to me and she's making
bread or canning moose or something equally
terrific. But Munroe. It's afternoon and he's
watching television. He doesn't even look up
when we're introduced. Rude old bugger, I
think but hating it just as much that he's
watching TV instead of trimming wicks or
milking some creature. We leave and on the
way to the truck I can hear him yelling at his
grandson, "Don't lick that cat. You'll get
leukemia".

His name is Gordon, Harry. This school
teacher guy. Gord. I don't like his name one
bit. Monday night I was over at his place for
the first time. It's all cleaned up which it
probably is anyway but I still like it, this
making me feel special. He's cooked
jackfish, wrapped up in some kind of leaves.
Baked apples.

His place is all cedar and just half-done
because he bought from Wilson who went
bankrupt like you said he would. Gordon is
determined with me. Serious as a machine.

The smell of wood makes me crazy. First
winter with you in that cabin? Because we're
just married I don't care a damn at first that
we've built this little box to live in with wood
that's green as lettuce. And that you stick to
the wall everytime you touch it. That there's
no power or water and nearly no windows.
That making coffee means half a day's work.
But then I begin to notice everything; nothing
is smooth, it's dark all the time, my clothes
are alive with sawdust and the walls are alive
with sap. So it starts. Small at first but
eventually this enormous longing, desperate
and ashamed. I want to live in a trailer. I
need to live in a mobile home.

Gordon asked me to stay overnight. But I
didn't. Or maybe I'm telling you lies again.
Maybe I got him drunk on rye and coke; sex
crazed widow flattens new-comer. You know
I don't think I ever lied to you once the
whole time we were together. But now,
Jesus. I did this when I was little too, make
up stuff to put in my diary.

But this, Harry, is the goods on Gordon.
This is a story that's true. I didn't stay
overnight but I did go to bed with him. I'm
just telling you, not asking permission. It
was alright. The best part being those very
pure times when thinking stops. Just touch,
react. But the flipside is thinking at a million
miles an hour. How it is still your body that
I know better than my own. How being held

by living arms, hands, brings home what a
body must be like lifeless. All the women
wanted the bodies found, all the families of
the victims. I never thought it'd be like that.
You'd think lost would be better than dead.
A strand of hope, invisible thin. But it makes
you crazy, never knowing a hundred percent.
It was way harder in the long run.

I am glad of meeting Gordon. Gord. I'm
not saying you two would've hit it off in a
huge way but I do like him, Harry. It's quite
wonderful to have that small leap in the gut
again when I know he's coming over, that
kind of thing.

Wolf thinks of him as a minor God. Just lies
at his feet with his paws up in the air like he's
waiting to be sacrificed or trying to
communicate telepathically that's he's trapped
in a trailer with a maniac.

Wolf and me went for a walk on Sunday
down to the lake. You know what he's
doing? Sniffing around and making circles.
Peeing on everything in sight and acting like a
general lunatic. I'm explaining to him that
it's February for God's sake and all the bears
are asleep and to quit being so damn antsy.
Then it dawns on me — he's still looking for
your scent. I mean it's been three years but
Wolf's still after your scent. And of course
everything is froze solid and you can't smell a
thing but whatever. Wolf is thinking you're
around every corner, maybe skidding out
birch for the woodpile or ice fishing or I
don't know what dogs think.

So we get to the shore and there's these three
kids from the reserve skating out on the lake.
Boys, maybe seven years old. Needless to
say, Wolf is scared of them. He stands on
the shore rocking back and forth, quivering
like a race horse. These kids are banging
around a soccer ball with these big plastic
baseball bats. Wolf is dying to get out there.
He wants to run and bark and fool around
with those kids and just be a regular dog.
But he can't do it. He just stays there and
yelps, does a few circles around me. And for
once I don't give him shit. I just pat his head
and let him be. Poor old Wolf. Just wanting
to be a regular dog. Everyone else wanting
him to be that way too. But Wolf's got a few
things figured out. He knows his limits.
Feels real good about those pats on the head.

So we just sat there for a long time, watching
those kids skate and the sun going down. I
love that time of day in winter. Used to be I
hated the night coming but it's alright now. I
mean it's not out-and-out terror anymore.
Not all the time at least.

Just a few more things, Harry. Then I'm
going to bed. They finally got me going to
another widows' group at the Elks twice a
month. In Newfoundland, they've got a
group just for Ranger families and it's
supposed to be great. But this bunch, I don't
know. There's a couple of new ones there
who are in a very bad way and it is good to
talk things out with them... support your
sisters, that kind of stuff. But there's this
one woman there, she's from town, works at
the Bay, around your mum's age. And she
says that widowhood, it's like checking into a

motel for one night. One night that lasts the
rest of your life. I mean let's face it. The
Elks is about the most depressing way to
spend an evening that's ever been invented.

Then this lady says that nothing feels like
home anymore. It's like we're all just waiting
to get to another place. And I thought —
right. Not that I think I'm going to another
place. It's just that it feels like that... the
waiting.

You know how when you stay in a motel
everything looks different — the bed, the
pattern on the carpet? Even some dumb old
TV show that you've watched every night of
your life seems nearly exotic when you're in a
motel. Very new.

Or those summers in Calgary before I met
you. I had this really terrible job in an
insurance office. Really punching the clock.
Working in this little room without any
windows. But every Friday at ten o'clock I'd
have to go to the Treasury Branch. And I'd
step out onto Centre Street and the world
looked different: the bus stop right out
front, even the way people walked.
Everything transformed and clear and
spooky, all at the same time.

So maybe that lady had a point, but she
hasn't figured out the whole thing completely.
I mean the world certainly does feel like a
motel just in that everything looks so
different. But you know Harry? Part of me
likes that. It makes a walk with Wolf or just
making dinner nearly miraculous.

I know. When we went to visit my folks and
on the way down we stayed in Edmonton in
that rather swanky place. We fooled around,
practically overdosed on Cable TV. And we
got room service for breakfast, opened the
curtains up really wide and there's this
apartment across the way. We watched all
these people run around and get ready for
work. The window's acting like a magnifying
glass, everyone looks bigger than life. Even
the air is defined and lively, just sparkling
with light.

Okay. Sometimes I do feel like I'm just
visiting here or stuck on the shore like old
Wolf, not really able to get involved in
anything. And very, very scared of going out
on the ice again.

But I'll tell you something. I am beginning to
feel again and part of me just loves staying in
a motel. So maybe it's because I'm so much
younger than most of them at the Elks but
I'm not just waiting, not anymore. Not held
down by that sadness. I mean I know it's
part of me but it can't run the show forever.
(looking at ring) What do you think of that?
My perfect jewel.

And what that lady from the Bay doesn't
know or anybody else is that you got through
to me. Valentine's through the ages. 1982.

You are about to slam, face first, into such a
storm. But not yet. Maybe it's still quiet out
there, just for a moment. I hope so. Wolf
and me have been down at the barn, checking
on things. I mean the animals would have to
be doing something absolutely bizarre for us

to see anything wrong but whatever. It's just
before noon. I come in the kitchen, the
radio's on. And there it is. First one out of
the gate, a Valentine's message, short and
sweet and probably sent the day before but
meant to be mine now. I carry it around
inside, hold onto it all day. It sends me to
bed warm. Loud and clear. You love me.
You got through.

Then late that night another message, hand
delivered by an embarrassed RCMP. The rig
has been evacuated. The constable offers to
wait with me. They will call again in an hour
on his car radio. I apologize for not having a
phone, for all his trouble. I make tea. Wolf
has gone wild. He can't believe his good
luck. All this activity in the middle of the
night.

Evacuated. What does it mean? Bombed out
villages, buildings. Living in an air raid
shelter. Living. He has left the rig and is in
a life boat. There is a bad storm, a fifty foot
sea.

How high? Like a grain elevator, fir tree.
No. Too tall. I know. Me and Lucy are at
Uncle Ray's, spitting down from the loft to
where the cowshit is, "You kids get the hell
down from there. You want to fall fifty feet
and land on your heads?" That's when I
know. Anything that big and made out of
water is a deadly thing. But don't think it or
it will be true and my fault. My legs are
weak as bread. I grab hold of the counter
and the kitchen floor moves like a raft
underneath me. And there you are, clear as
ice for a single moment. In a little boat,
wearing that awful parka from Sears.

The horn on the police car blasts out of
nowhere. Twice. Wolf and the police go to
get the message on the radio phone. And I
know it again but don't believe it for a
second. Not on your life. I should go to
Munroe's because your mother believes in
God and I don't. I didn't mean it. The
RCMP catches me down on my knees on the
cold lineoleum. He shakes his head. This is
very hard for him, trying to tell me that my
husband is dead.

But he doesn't tell me that. He says the rig
has gone down and two of the lifeboats but
the third boat is still out there. That means
you. I know it.

But then this cop tells me they said not to
have much hope. And I slap him across the
back of the head.

I should have listened to him. It would've
made the next few days a lot easier. All that
waiting and glued to the radio. I should go
to Newfoundland but I'm afraid of flying
now, of moving, of leaving the ground. Then
the names of the dead are just read over the
radio, in Munroe's kitchen. Confirmed. At
the service, someone from your company is
there telling me how sad this has made him.
What I don't realize at the time is he can't
apologize because it might make them liable.
If you'd worked for Mobil itself, they
wouldn't even have tried to make contact
after the accident. Just hear it on the news
with everyone else.

It doesn't start for a week or so because I
suppose I'm in shock but I relive your death
for a long, long time. You're in the lifeboat
that nearly made it. That's what all the
widows think. We think alike. I can't go
through that stuff anymore.

Nearly midnight, Harry. Valentine's through
the ages is coming to a close. Remember how
I told you that first message sent me to bed
warm? It's still there. A little bit.

MARJORIE *removes the ring from her
finger and leaves it on the table.*

But wearing this forever. I don't know. I
don't think it's such a great idea anymore.
Does that make sense? I hope so. It does for
me and I guess that's the important part.

It always felt so mean that it had to be
Valentine's Day, that it was the last day you
were alive. But I'm not so sure anymore.

This is what I'm sure of. You loved me.
You got through.

The End